I0066699

SMALL BALL
BIG
Dreams

Praise for *Small Ball Big Dreams*

"*Small Ball Big Dreams* is a must read for all those who aspire for greatness in leadership and excellence in performance. Joel Goldberg's many stories weave a moral compass based on faith, hope, love, integrity, and trust. Words such as courage, persistence, fortitude, pay it forward, and mentoring roll from story to story. A great read by a gifted storyteller and an exceptional motivational speaker. Joel Goldberg has another winner!"

Terry Dunn, Retired President & CEO,
JE Dunn Construction Group

"What has always impressed me about Joel, right after his tasteful selection in clothing, is how much heart he puts into his broadcasting. That heart is on full display in *Small Ball Big Dreams* as he writes about amazing people and the humanity at their core."

Joe Posnanski, former *Sports Illustrated* and *The Kansas City Star* columnist and author of nine books

"There are many valuable lessons in this book about people and life that really resonate. It's about dreaming big and harnessing the power of your dreams to make them a reality. It's about valuing the journey to achieving your dreams—especially the small steps. It's about family, the family members you grow up with and the ones you add along the way. It's about experiences that will forever shape your life. The stories that unfold with every page in *Small Ball Big Dreams* will touch your heart and leave you with lessons you can live by. Joel really knocked it out of the park with this book!"

Lisa Ginter, CEO, CommunityAmerica Credit Union

"From Lorenzo Cain's work ethic to overcome a late start—having never played baseball until a coach needed one more player to fill a JV roster Lorenzo's sophomore year, to Kevin Youkilis's non-stop hustle for shelf space and building the right 'locker room chemistry' for his craft brewing company, to Tech N9ne finding his life's purpose to pursue music to deliver his 'fan psychiatrist's' healing messages, those looking for inspiring lessons on how to succeed in their business career need look no further than Joel Goldberg's *Small Ball Big Dreams*."

Dan Hesse, Chairman-Akamai and Former CEO-Sprint

"Nearly every big dream that comes true begins with never giving up. Joel Goldberg hits it out of the park again with his new book *Small Ball Big Dreams*. Each chapter will remind the reader that every small, determined, methodical step toward achieving big, audacious dreams in your life is worth it. Even further, Joel shows with each featured story that journeys can be dreams themselves."

Greg Graves, Retired CEO & Chairman, Burns & McDonnell

"What makes *Small Ball Big Dreams* stand out is how Joel connects personal stories to bigger lessons that anyone can relate to—whether you're a leader, a team player, or someone trying to make a difference. It shows that even small steps can lead to big things, and that chasing after a purpose is a journey worth taking. This book isn't just for baseball fans or businesspeople; it's for anyone who believes that even the smallest moments can hold big dreams."

Claudia Meyer, President and CEO of Cristo Rey Kansas City

"Joel Goldberg has the uncanny ability to take the stories of the ballplayers and baseball executives he has met along his journey as one of America's truly gifted baseball broadcasters and share them with the reader as if we were actually there. His gift as a storyteller is on full display in this fascinating compilation of stories, each of them told in a Pregame, Game, and Post-Game format. *Small Ball Big Dreams* is Joel Goldberg's 'broadcast about life' from a baseball perspective. The book is a tape-measure home run!"

Mark Goldston, Executive Chairman of The Beachbody Company
and General Partner of Athletic Propulsion Labs (APL)

SMALL BALL
BIG
Dreams

JOEL GOLDBERG

INDIE BOOKS
INTERNATIONAL

SMALL BALL **BIG** *Dreams*

© 2025 Joel Goldberg

All rights reserved.

Printed in the United States of America.

No part of this publication may be reproduced or distributed in any form or by any means, without the prior permission of the publisher. Requests for permission should be directed to permissions@indiebooksintl.com, or mailed to Permissions, Indie Books International, 2511 Woodlands Way, Oceanside, CA 92054.

The views and opinions in this book are those of the author at the time of writing this book, and do not reflect the opinions of Indie Books International or its editors.

Neither the publisher nor the author is engaged in rendering legal or other professional services through this book. If expert assistance is required, the services of appropriate professionals should be sought. The publisher and the author shall have neither liability nor responsibility to any person or entity with respect to any loss or damage caused directly or indirectly by the information in this publication.

Super Bowl® is a registered trademark of the NFL Properties, LLC

Energizer® is a registered trademark of Energizer Brands, LLC

Lyrics from "Like I Ain't" and "KCMO Anthem" are used with permission from Tech N9ne and Strange Music, Inc.

ISBN-13: 978-1-966168-01-0
Library of Congress Control Number: 2024924005

Designed by Melissa Farr, Back Porch Creative, LLC

INDIE BOOKS INTERNATIONAL®, INC.
2511 WOODLANDS WAY
OCEANSIDE, CA 92054
www.indiebooksintl.com

Contents

Foreword

vividly remember the day I made my MLB debut. I had been playing AAA ball in Omaha when my manager showed up at my apartment. "You're going to the big leagues," he said and told me not to worry: I wouldn't be in that night's starting lineup. A few hours later, I landed in Chicago for the first time in my life. I hailed a cab—with bats in tow—and arrived in the locker room about an hour before game time. Imagine my surprise when I learned I would actually be batting 8th.

For a kid who had only set his sights on professional baseball a few years prior, it was—in many ways—a dream come true. I had always known I wanted to be some sort of athlete, but that was not the path I expected my career to take. In fact, I'd hoped to play through college before realizing there weren't any teams knocking on my door with scholarship offers. The last thing I anticipated was being drafted in the second round by the Kansas City Royals. That's the funny thing about dreams. Sometimes, you choose them; other times, they choose you.

It's something Joel Goldberg understands well. Anyone who has seen him in his element—broadcasting a game or on stage speaking—can appreciate the obvious skill he brings to his craft. What I have always admired most about Joel is his intuitive way of connecting with others.

He's honest and accurate, without negativity. That can be tough to do in a game where success is defined by failures. But more importantly, he enjoys the process. And as I always say, it's easier to be successful when you're having fun.

Small Ball Big Dreams showcases Joel doing what he does best: connecting as a storyteller. Using stories of notable figures in sports, business, and beyond, he recounts the little plays each of them made to get to and stay at the top. Some are underdog successes, and others are personal triumphs of new dreams that replace old ones. Every one of them draws you in, and offers a lesson that resonates universally.

Baseball, like business, is about hitting the ball hard every chance you get. Some swings will be misses, others will be outs. But every now and then, you hear the crack of a ball flying out of the park. And there's nothing sweeter than when it all comes together, and you achieve what you had been working toward all along.

George Brett
MLB Hall of Fame Class of 1999

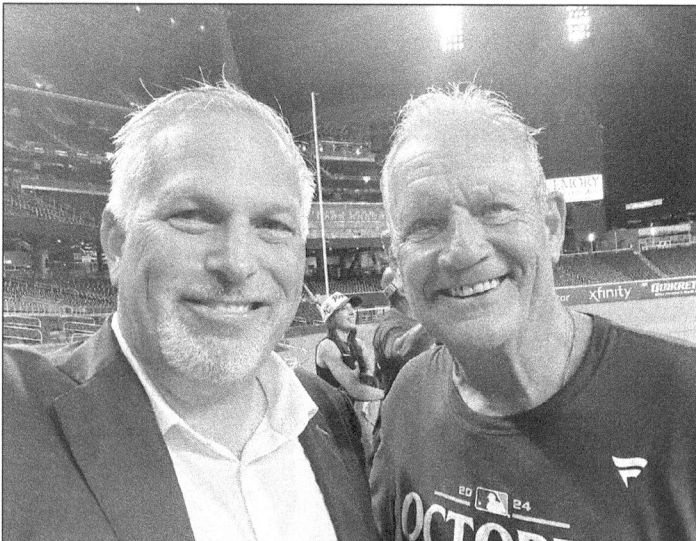

Introduction

Bobby Witt Jr. walked over to me as 25,178 fans remained in their seats to hear from the emerging young superstar before watching the Friday fireworks. Moments earlier, the phenom smoked a triple down the line to send the crowd into a frenzy, tying a game against Seattle that had seen Kansas City losing 8-0. One play after Witt's triple, he crossed the plate to complete the improbable comeback. As the twenty-three-year-old star approached me, still breathing heavily from his triple and the mad dash home, I told my producer, Kevin Cedergren, to give us a second before starting the interview that would go out live to our television audience and to all the fans in the stadium.

I wanted him to give him the chance to catch his breath and his thoughts, so I asked, "Need a second?"

He replied, "No, let's do it."

Nothing seems to ever fluster the kid. I could feel the adrenaline pouring out of him as his breath still raced at a pace that matched his elite sprinting speed. As the interview started, I asked him how they pulled off the unthinkable win. He simply turned to the amped-up crowd and answered by posing a question to an audience hanging on every word.

"I don't know, what do y'all think? Pretty fun," he said with his slight Texas drawl.

That sent the fan base to another level of euphoria, and I knew from my thirty years of broadcast experience to wait for the booming ovation to die before resuming the discussion. Fifteen seconds later, as the cheers began to fade, they ramped up again with chants of "Bobby, Bobby," and I waited longer. He pumped his fist to the crowd as a massive smile spread across his face. This generational talent soaked it all in. A half a minute of pandemonium finally ended, and Witt was doused with back-to-back celebratory sports drink bucket splashes before I resumed the interview. Witt admitted he couldn't speak in the moment. I was told later the crowd's response choked him up.

During the interview, he summed up his feelings by saying, "These are the things I go home and dream about."

Never underestimate the power of a dream. It's a powerful phrase I share with audiences across the country when I deliver keynote speeches about winning trust and building culture. My business coach, Mark LeBlanc, encouraged me to pursue the meaning behind these words and sent me down this path within moments of finishing my first book, *Small Ball Big Results*.

"I have the title for your next book," he told me.

As my mind raced, I thought, *The ink has barely dried on the printing of book one,* but Mark suggested *Small Ball Big Dreams*. It dawned on me in the moment that we all dream—athletes, business owners, executives, entrepreneurs, or any profession. And I've lived a dream career interviewing others about their dreams.

In *Small Ball Big Results*, I highlighted the little things that lead to success. As a longtime television reporter and host with more than half of my career spent covering baseball, I knew that the real-life version of bunting, stealing bases, and advancing the runner, also known on the diamond as "small ball," were the soft skills that make people successful. Dreams do come true. We usually see the result of those dreams, but how often do we focus on the small steps taken along the journey? And when do those dreams ever go as planned?

Like most kids who loved sports growing up, I dreamed of starring for my hometown team, the Philadelphia Phillies, as a boy in South Jersey. But I realized that my prowess of hitting home runs while playing little league and backyard wiffle ball would take me as far as the local ballfield and no further. The next best option was talking about it, and visions of stepping in front of the camera with a microphone became my obsession as an early teen. My first and second grade teacher, Mrs. Dunwoody, told my parents that I regularly disrupted class to let everyone know about the details of a baseball, basketball, football, hockey, or soccer game the night before. I used to daydream about how cool it would be to go to games for my job and get paid. I think I would've even done it for free. Or maybe I could be the local sports anchor on the news? That was my dream, but I could never envision seventeen years as the television pregame and postgame show host and in-game reporter for the Kansas City Royals. Sideline reporters and postgame show hosts barely existed when I was growing up. How can we dream of jobs that have yet to be created?

As Anita Newton, Chief Innovation Officer at Community America Credit Union, told me on my podcast in March 2022, "Young people who are in school today, whether five or fifteen, will graduate from college and go after jobs that haven't even been invented yet."

Drone operator? Driverless car engineer? Ecosystem lawyer? The world has changed and will continue to do so. I certainly had no plans of hosting a podcast in the 1970s and '80s. No such thing existed, yet my podcast, *Rounding the Bases*, has given me the opportunity to talk about people's dreams on and off the baseball field. It's allowed me to do what I love best: storytelling.

One of the privileges of having a presence on television as well as a podcasting platform is the ability to share stories from inside the locker room and the board room and sometimes just help elevate a cause. Of course, not all dreams come true, and my heart sank during a podcast interview with a woman named Meghan in January 2022. I decided to produce a four-part series on human trafficking. Meghan shared memories of a gut-wrenching and painful childhood of being trafficked by her father. When I asked her a simple question about her dreams and aspirations as a kid, she told me she didn't have the ability to dream and didn't know how to envision a future. She couldn't think ahead to the next year or even the next day. Meghan is a hero and survivor and now speaks to law enforcement along with Dan Nash and Alison Phillips, the two co-founders of the Human Trafficking Training Center. They were my guides to enlightening my audience on this critical issue and introduced me to Meghan. She's now a training instructor and victim advocate with real dreams.

"It's a gift every day that I'm alive, that I survived things I probably shouldn't have, and that I get to do life with people who are walking through some hard stuff," Meghan told me. "It fulfills my heart, and my dream is just to help other people have the ability to dream."

I was lucky enough to grow up in a household where I could dream about a television career, wanting one day to be the great Bob Costas. As a twenty-one-year-old TV intern in Memphis in the summer of 1993, I met my idol at a minor league All-Star Game. He was a celebrity coach, and I nervously told him, "I hope one day to be half as good as you," whatever that meant. Twenty-nine years later, I moderated a panel discussion in Cooperstown, New York, during Major League Baseball (MLB) Hall of Fame weekend in the summer of 2022. I spent the weekend covering the induction of Negro Leagues legend Buck O'Neil, and the panel of guests included Costas. He agreed to be my guest on *Rounding the Bases* and appeared on an episode a few months later, sharing his dreams of wanting to talk about sports once he realized he could not play at an elite level. It was a pinch-myself moment, topped by my arrival at Yankee Stadium in September 2024 to broadcast a Royals-Yankees game for the Kansas City telecast. Standing outside the visiting clubhouse was the legendary Costas, preparing to announce the game nationally on MLB Network. As I saw him, he called out my name and offered a hug. I've lived in a world where meeting famous people and covering superstars is normal, and it's just work to me now. I try never to take it for granted, but the Costas moment at Yankee Stadium reminded me to keep savoring those dreams.

This book is filled with stories about star athletes, role players, and heroes that I hope will inspire you. Never underestimate the power of a dream.

1

Lorenzo Cain

PREGAME

"Are you crying? There's no crying," Tom Hanks's character Jimmy Dugan shouted to a weeping Evelyn Gardner, played by Bitty Schram in the 1992 classic *A League of Their Own*. "There's no crying in baseball!" It's an iconic scene, but I've seen enough tears in sports to know there is indeed crying in baseball.

As a former star athlete told us on our *Royals Live* pregame show in early May 2023, "Tonight I'm going to try my best not to shed a tear. I'm going to try my best to stay strong."

Lorenzo Cain stepped onto the field after his interview with us for a ceremony to honor his retirement and addressed a festive crowd. As the fans gave the outfielder a standing ovation, Cain covered his eyes and wept. His young sons ran up to console their father. He collected himself and cried again. And again. His best effort to contain his emotions lasted all of a few seconds. It seemed like everyone in attendance that night suffered from eye-watering allergies.

GAME

Lorenzo Cain thrived on center stage in the biggest moments. His elite-level athleticism was matched by one of the most radiant smiles in baseball. Yet if truth be told, he preferred to blend into the background. But on the special occasion of his retirement, Cain basked in the glory of putting on a Kansas City Royals jersey one last time, wearing his number six jersey a final time after signing a one-day contract for ceremonial purposes to retire as a Royal. The emotions overwhelmed the man known in KC as Lo Cain. It was the celebration of a journey he could have never envisioned when he began high school in Madison, Florida, about fifteen miles south of the Florida-Georgia state line.

Most big leaguers I talk to grew up hitting walk-off home runs in the neighborhood while fantasizing about being a World Series hero. There's no greater joy in my job than interviewing a pro athlete on the day he makes his MLB debut. I always tell him to soak in the moment and that whether he has the greatest performance or a tough first game, he will forever be a big leaguer and never forget that initial appearance.

When a young outfielder named Nate Eaton stepped to the plate in his first MLB game in Toronto, he struck out in the second inning. Flyouts in the fourth and seventh meant the twenty-five-year-old was hitless with one more possible at-bat looming. He and many teammates weren't supposed to be there that night. Canadian law prohibited visitors from crossing the border without a COVID vaccine in 2022, and teams across baseball were forced to leave unvaccinated players in the United States. Kansas City's roster included ten such players, meaning numerous prospects would suit up as replacements for the four games at Rogers Centre. Many, like Eaton, had never played at the highest level. Eaton received one more chance in the ninth inning. His team led 2-1 and needed an extra run for insurance against a dangerous Blue Jays team. The oddsmakers pegged the Royals as the largest underdog of any game in baseball so far that season because nearly half of the roster was made up of minor leaguers. Eaton stood crouched in the batter's box, full count, one out, as he intently looked at the left-handed pitcher. This would be the tenth pitch of a long, grinding plate appearance. The eighty-seven miles per hour offering was thrown down the middle of the plate, and Eaton connected. Anthony Banda, the southpaw on the mound, turned on contact, watched the hit sail, and squatted down, bracing for the end. The ball flew over the left field wall and Eaton stoically rounded the bases before breaking out a massive smile as he crossed home plate while pointing to the stands.

It would be their only win of the four-game series, and it was a moment Eaton would never forget. As my star of the game, he reflected during our live televised interview on the field, never losing his grin as his teammates doused him with ice-cold water.

"It's everything I dreamed of growing up, simulating in the backyard, everything with your friends. It's a dream come true," Eaton told me.

As for tears, I know my broadcast colleagues had them in the booth and I did on the field when we heard his next comment.

"When I was running around the bases, right as I got to second, the only person I could hear cheering was my mom." Who couldn't relate to that?

Like Eaton, Cain's mom meant everything to him. But unlike Eaton, Lorenzo did not dream of baseball early in life. Reflecting on his childhood, he said, "A young Lo Cain was just hanging out at the house. I'm doing chores, hanging around with my cousins and friends, and playing any kind of sport I can, just in the backyard . . . But the road to organized sports was definitely later on in my future. I guess better late than never."

Young Lorenzo was usually picked last when playing sports with his brothers and cousins in the neighborhood. Being the youngest built a fearlessness and ability to compete. He returned home every night as darkness settled in, covered in dirt and sweat from playing, unaware that the lessons learned trying to compete at a higher level would serve him well later in life as he eventually embarked on a professional baseball career. His understanding of hard work and the importance of staying humble came from Patricia, his single-parent mom, who worked two jobs to support her children. He can thank his mother for inadvertently sending him to baseball stardom. Lorenzo wanted to play football, but Patricia put her foot down, unwilling to let her boy suit up on the gridiron, believing the sport to be too dangerous. He tried out for the basketball team as a freshman in high school and was cut.

"I said, hey, what's left? Baseball. So I decided to take a stab at it," Cain said.

Lorenzo inquired about playing his sophomore year and received a warm welcome from the coach, who said adding another player, even one with no formal training, would enable the junior varsity team to avoid canceling the season due to low numbers.

"I basically showed up with some basketball shoes. I had some jean shorts on and a collared shirt."

He borrowed equipment from friends and coaches, but a lack of gear couldn't prevent Lorenzo from being the best in one category from the start. He was the fastest on the field. Hitting, on the other hand, was a different story. How could he know then that he would one day hit three home runs in one game at Yankee Stadium?

As he embarked on a high school baseball career, young Lo showed up for baseball tryouts having only used a metal bat and tennis ball in his backyard. For the longest time he couldn't even hit a ball out of the infield. Hoping to improve, he began bypassing lunch at school to hit off a machine. The kid who would eventually earn a Gold Glove for his elite outfield play in the majors began as a third baseman before switching to left field. He made varsity as a junior but played sparingly. Prior to his senior year of high school, he committed to taking his game to the next level, not with the thought of playing in college or being drafted to play pro ball. His motivation stemmed from his disdain for sitting on the bench. Pride can be a powerful trait and Cain mimicked the work ethic he learned from his mom. Being coachable and willing to handle criticism also helped. His athleticism and raw skills made him a project, but one that began drawing the attention of evaluators.

Cain's senior year, the letters poured in, expressing interest, and the Milwaukee Brewers selected him with the 496th overall pick of the 2004 player draft.

He laughed at the memory: "I didn't even know it was draft day. They called my house and said, 'Hey, we drafted you in the seventeenth round,' and I remember just hanging up the phone saying, 'Okay, thank you.'"

His mom asked about the phone call, and he told her someone had said they had drafted him.

"I just was clueless about the entire situation. I didn't know anything about baseball. I knew that I was tired of going home every day doing chores. I wanted to be a part of something."

Cain made his MLB debut on July 16, 2010, for the Milwaukee Brewers and played in forty-three games that season at baseball's highest level, excited about the possibility of taking steps forward the next season. The path of his career changed months later when Milwaukee traded him to Kansas City during the offseason. Pain would set in quickly at the thought of being unable to make a name for himself with the team that drafted him. After receiving numerous calls from his mother on a December morning in 2010 to inform him about the news she saw on TV, Lorenzo, in disbelief, turned on ESPN to see his name across the ticker. Cy Young award-winner Zack Greinke and shortstop Yuniesky Betancourt were traded by the Kansas City Royals to the Milwaukee Brewers for Lorenzo Cain, Alcides Escobar, Jeremy Jeffress, and Jake Odorizzi—a blockbuster move that would change the trajectory of the Royals, the Kansas City area, and Cain.

Looking back on the trade more than a decade later, he told me, "I had mixed emotions. I didn't know what to expect. I didn't know what to think . . . it ended up basically being the best career move I could've ever wished for."

Cain's KC stardom hardly developed overnight. More time in the minor leagues and injuries became a part of the painful growth process. His elite athleticism began to show regularly in 2013 at the big-league level. By 2014, Lo Cain and a group of relative unknowns nationally became household names in America's Heartland. His speed, power, and elite defense made him a force. He fit in well with a young and energetic team that would capture the hearts of a region by breaking a twenty-nine-year playoff drought. While Cain could be the best player on the field on any night, he gladly avoided the spotlight.

Polite and almost always smiling, Lorenzo remained content, letting his play do the talking, until one game in Detroit in 2014. Something changed in him that day. It was a moment best described as the kid at school finally confronting the bully for continuously stealing his lunch money. Cain stood up to the bully, aka the Detroit Tigers, at Comerica Park. Detroit had regularly beat the Royals and everyone else.

"They're crushing everybody. And they're destroying us. You just sometimes feel like you didn't have a chance. That's how good they were," Cain told me.

After a hit, Cain stood on the bag watching Tigers star first-baseman Victor Martinez laughing and basking in the glory of beating up on the "little guy." When Martinez said hi to Lorenzo, Cain decided no more and broke into an expletive-laden tirade few teammates knew existed in him.

"Sometimes you just get fed up getting your face kicked in all the time and that's what they did to us. Flat-out bullies, took our lunch money, took our candy. And, you know, I'm the type of guy, I'm not a fan of bullies." He laughed at the memory, continuing, "I don't know exactly what I said, Joel, but I know I was just yelling out a bunch of words that I probably shouldn't be saying. But at the end of the day, enough was enough. And I was sick of them beating us."

I will forever remember the Royals first-base coach Rusty Kuntz, Cain's mentor, making a beeline after the game to the back of the team bus, where the broadcasters sat.

"You guys won't believe what happened with Lo Cain," Kuntz glowingly told us about Cain's outburst.

Cain felt that moment was the turning point for the team and him.

"I remember just coming with an attitude that I think we needed as a group. It also helped me lock in. I've always played better when I was angry."

Detroit won the division that year, one game better than Kansas City, but the Royals made the playoffs, earning a spot in the one-game wildcard. They won a thriller in the wildcard, then upset the Los Angeles Angels with a sweep completed on the same day the Baltimore Orioles eliminated the Tigers. KC then shocked Baltimore by winning all four games to take the American League pennant. No one had more hits in the series than Cain, who was named the American League Championship Series MVP.

A game-seven loss to San Francisco in the World Series ended the small market Cinderella story. Cain called it heartbreaking, but the underdog Royals took the gut punch and responded. None of the so-called experts predicted a follow-up performance in 2015. Kansas City, led in part by the heart of Cain, saw otherwise. Lorenzo received the first clue of what would come next in spring training the following February.

"I've never seen every single person show up in shape ready to go," Cain told me, recognizing that a few players on every team usually report with some catching up to do after ignoring their diets or the weight room. "I think from day one of spring training to the end of the season, we were all locked in and ready to rock."

The kid who never played organized baseball until his sophomore year of high school became an All-Star and World Series champion in 2015. He even finished third in the American League MVP voting for the season. When Cain's contract expired two years later, he signed a lucrative deal with Milwaukee, of all teams, and finished his career in Wisconsin where he started.

POSTGAME

In the end, Lorenzo Cain played thirteen MLB seasons—seven with the Royals and six with the Brewers. He chose to officially retire as a Royal and say goodbye in front of the fans he called family. His mother, wife, three sons, in-laws, and others sat in chairs on the field at Kauffman Stadium, watching the tributes and gifts flow as fast as the tears of everyone in attendance. They even gave Lo Cain a cane, poking fun at a man who always seemed to limp around the locker room hurt before magically healing in time to dazzle in the outfield.

The game began late because Lorenzo struggled to speak at the podium, overcome with emotions. So much for not crying.

"It all just kind of hit me at once," he said after the tears finally dried up. The family, friends, impact, and joy he brought were beyond his wildest dreams. Lorenzo Cain was the epitome of small ball: an unselfish teammate capable of hitting home runs and playing the superstar role but always willing to excel at the little things. He is proof that anything is possible.

"Even though you showed up late to the party, always put in the work necessary to be great at what you're trying to achieve . . . having a mindset of, you can do it; you can go out and get it done. Even if you fail, get up and try again. And never give up on yourself."

2

Suzyn Waldman

PREGAME

I'm not sure I've met a baseball announcer who seemingly knows everyone like the energetic, always-on-the-move Suzyn Waldman.

"When you say I know everybody, I don't know everybody, but I know people who do know everybody," she told me on my podcast in 2022.

She's humble, but my eyes don't lie. Every time the Yankees face the Royals, I watch her work the clubhouse, gathering details and passing on information about the players. I often say that I keep getting older, and the athletes I cover keep getting younger. When I began working with the Royals, I was in my thirties, ten years older than the players. Now in my fifties, I'm connecting with the next generation of twentysomethings every day. Suzyn is still mastering it in her seventies. The Yankees radio color commentator is an inspiration to women who are finally making progress after being ignored for generations in sports broadcasting. But it's not just the amazing women in my profession who try to be like her.

I find myself wanting to emulate Suzyn, too, because she's a master storyteller. I watched her track down Kansas City's twenty-four-year-old first baseman Nick Pratto to polish a story before the game one night.

Then on to Jose Cuas, the former-FedEx-driver-turned-Royals-reliever and winner of the Tony Conigliaro Award. It's given to a "Major Leaguer who has overcome adversity through the attributes of spirit, determination, and courage that were trademarks of Tony C." the former Red Sox outfielder whose career was cut short by a beanball in 1967. Conigliaro passed in 1990, and Suzyn was a friend of Tony C's. She wanted to make sure Cuas knew about the man before he played at Fenway later that summer because he would be asked about it by the Boston media. Of course, she knew Tony C. She knows everybody.

As I watched her at work and listened back to her appearance on my podcast, *Rounding the Bases*, I thought to myself, *I've done this a long time, and I have so much room for improvement.* Suzyn Waldman is proof it's never too late to chase a dream.

GAME

Suzyn Waldman attended Red Sox games as a kid. Dreams of broadcasting for the Yankees? No chance. Nor the Sox or any team, for that matter.

"I grew up in the '50s. I mean, there were no women doing this. You never thought about it."

Sitting and chatting with Suzyn in the Yankees radio booth on a Sunday morning in July 2023, I told her I wanted to write a chapter about her in this book. I passed on the story of my mom, and when I shared the challenge my mother faced in being told she had two options, Suzyn finished my sentence.

"Teacher or nurse," she said, not the least bit surprised about the limited options. Her early career path resembled my mom's as far as an interest in the arts, and like my mother, Suzyn also started a second act later in her thirties that never fit her childhood dreams. She loved all sports but aspired to sing and act on Broadway, which she did.

"I worked a lot. I never became a star. I never became what I wanted to be. But I worked constantly. And as the music was changing, and I wasn't changing with it, I figured I'd better find something else to do. And I didn't want to be somebody's mother for the rest of my life on stage or to be the queen of revivals."

Her love of sports never diminished, and she managed to leverage her musical and theatric abilities into performances that eventually opened up a new stage.

"I always sang the national anthem in the '70s any place we were. It wasn't because I realized I was going to get on television. I just wanted to go to the ballgame wherever I was. And that was the way to do it for free."

One of her best friends, because Suzyn's always known people who know people, was longtime Red Sox announcer, the late Ken Coleman. Coleman introduced Waldman to the man creating WFAN in New York, the first twenty-four-hour all-sports radio station. Suggesting Suzyn knew more about sports than anyone he knew, Coleman encouraged her to submit a demo. Hired to do sports updates, Suzyn admits she had no idea what she was doing initially but thought she could figure it out. The criticism came immediately for a thirty-nine-year-old rookie who happened to be a woman when no women were in sports.

"I heard one of the owners of WFAN say, 'Get that smart aleck bleep off my air and afternoon drive, the one with the Boston accent, get her off.' And Jim Lampley was the host that day. It was the first day, and I looked up, and he said, 'Just keep going,' and that's what I did."

Like the Energizer Bunny, she kept going and going, even as she faced roadblocks every day. Not from players she covered at Yankees and Mets games, although there was some pushback, but more from her colleagues and competitors. She sat in the press box in Yankee Stadium in 1987 with no one talking to her for the full year.

"The radio people thought I was taking a job away from a real reporter, meaning male . . . I was middle-aged when I realized that nobody wanted women around in sports. And then it became, 'No, no, no, you're not going to tell me what to do.' Listen, I made it through twenty years of theater. I could do anything if I did that. Sports broadcasting makes theater look like nursery school."

She's tough and resilient but also human, meaning being the only woman then came with a price. In today's day and age, the disgusting comments aimed at so many of my female colleagues come via social media, a reminder that sexism and discrimination still exist in a world of progress. For Suzyn, she took it all as the lone woman, including death threats in 1998, which meant she needed a police detail.

"I'm still scared, scared to go into crowds. And I still wonder where that guy is . . . I was never alone, from the time I hit the players' parking lot till the time I left. And if I got to the players' parking lot and my car was started, that meant they got another bomb threat."

Yankees bullpen coach John Stearns used to start her car. To this day, she bumps into detectives who say, "Ms. Waldman, I just want you to know I was one of your guys back then." So many protected her that she couldn't name them all.

While most of her challenging times originated from the media, the players she covered accepted her and followed the lead of Yankees stars like Don Mattingly, Dave Winfield, Ron Guidry, and Dave Righetti, who embraced her. Going into other clubhouses didn't guarantee her that same protection. She remembers walking out of a clubhouse in Toronto in the 1980s, shunned by a Blue Jays player. Ira Berkow wrote about the moment in *The New York Times* on July 20, 1989:

Two years ago, Suzyn Waldman, of WFAN, was in the Toronto Blue Jays' locker room after an important game in the division race. Several reporters were interviewing George Bell, the Toronto left fielder. When Waldman moved into the group, Bell began to scream obscenities in Spanish and English about a woman in the locker room, and said he'd cut off the interview.

Waldman still recalls the details thirty-five years later, including the heartwarming elements displayed by one of Bell's teammates.

"As I'm walking out, trying not to cry, I hear this voice, and I turned around, and it was Jesse Barfield, who was the right fielder on Toronto. And he said, 'I went three for four today; don't you want to talk to me?'"

Toronto traded Barfield to the Yankees in 1989 and a lifelong friendship between Suzyn and the outfielder exists to this day. She continues to push forward, forging new connections daily at ballparks decades later. Always the performer, she never views any day as the same. The same could be said about theater, and while Broadway followed a script eight times a week, she found something different every time.

"It doesn't matter that you're saying the same lines; you have a different audience, you have different feedback, maybe the guy that you're talking to had a fight with his wife. So you have to react to that. It's the world you get up to every day. And it's never the same, or it shouldn't be the same. And all it is is in your mind. And so it never gets boring."

I told Suzyn I couldn't get up and sing or act on stage and would crumple in fear given that opportunity. My daughter Ellie has those skills, but not me. I sang "Take Me Out to the Ballgame" at Kauffman Stadium in 2008 and bombed. My lack of theatrical skills match my ability to hit a baseball (swing and a miss), yet it does not mean I'm incapable of taking a different stage as a storyteller. This, she pointed out, makes me a performer. And in a day of analytics, artificial intelligence, and the ability to have any information we want at our fingertips, the human element still matters in all professions.

"If we lose the stories, all we have is computer games out there," she passionately stated. "And you have to remember why do we cheer for people? Why do we want a team to win? How many people do you know that can tell you the stories of Whitey Herzog and the World Series, and the stories with the Yankee–Kansas City games and the fights on the field and all of that? That's what people remember forty years ago; that's what's important. And if it's just, 'Yeah, they won 4-2 and it was a pretty good game.' No, that isn't what keeps it going."

Suzyn's longevity in the game stems from her genuine interest in people. Her curiosity is a skill that applies to almost any profession. "I try and talk to almost everybody every day, not necessarily about the game."

Her passion, storytelling, and ability to connect with people are pure elements of small ball and the ability to hustle gave Suzyn's critics no choice but to respect her work. Filing reports during the 1989 Battle of the Bay World Series between the Oakland A's and San Francisco Giants amidst a massive earthquake earned her praise.

"That was the first time any writer ever took me seriously."

When a reporter can earn the respect of a major name like late Yankees owner George Steinbrenner, the competition must pay attention. No one in the media could take the elevator at old Yankee Stadium when Steinbrenner was using it, so Suzyn would run up and down the ramps to wait for the owner and ask questions when the door opened. Steinbrenner would fly into New York from his Florida home in the winter every year to host a lunch for beat reporters around Christmastime and Suzyn was not included. "Just the guys," she was told. Frozen out of the gathering but trying to find access and an advantage, she asked the head of sales at

WFAN how much money her regular Yankees report on the afternoon drive show sold for and how many people listened.

"It turned out more people listened to me at 5:05 than read every paper," Suzyn recalled.

Armed with these impressive numbers, she wrote Steinbrenner a letter one offseason, sharing her findings and telling him this is why he needed to talk to her. "I'm coming down to Tampa next week, and I want an interview," she wrote.

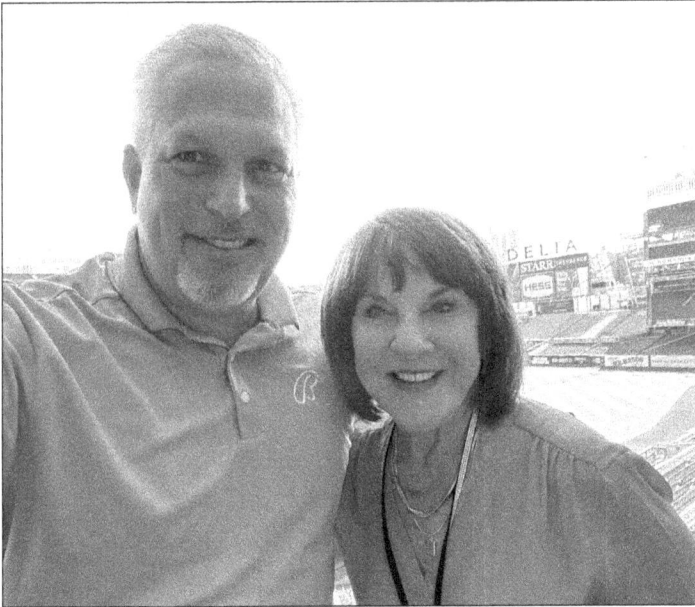

With no idea if he would oblige, Suzyn made the trip and received a phone call at her hotel from a woman.

"She says, 'It's Joanne, George Steinbrenner's secretary. He will see you tomorrow morning in the office at nine o'clock. And by the way, I have Xeroxed your letter, and I have sent it to every woman in the building.'"

Suzyn remembers what George told her the moment she arrived at his office. "He said, 'Waldman, I don't like women in sports. I don't like women firemen. I don't like women policemen. I want women to look pretty and spend my money,' and I said, 'Okay, I can do that. Now, about the pitching staff,' and he started laughing. And that was that."

He only called her by her first name when he was mad at her. "The Boss" could get nasty with her. "You're cut off," she remembers hearing more than once, but Suzyn holds him in the highest regard years after his passing in 2010.

"Except for my mother and grandfather, he was probably the most important person in my life."

Suzyn even played diplomat and peacemaker, helping end a more than decade-long feud between Yankees legend Yogi Berra and Steinbrenner in 1999.

"That was my present to George and my present to the New York Yankees because I am nowhere without George Steinbrenner."

Steinbrenner's opposition to women in sports would not fly in today's world. But that's not to say the game or world has finally evolved to an equal playing field. A 2021 game between the Tampa Bay Rays and Baltimore Orioles featured an all-women's broadcast crew. Heidi Watney and Lauren Gardner handled the pre- and postgame show hosting responsibilities. Melanie Newman called the action with Sarah Langs as her analyst, and Alanna Rizzo worked the sideline. A monumental and historic game, yet Waldman wondered *why not more*.

"I'm still the only one full-time in the booth . . . There are women all over the league that are fabulous. But I see them in little boxes. And as long as they stay in their little box, they're absolutely fine . . . I mean, the goal is not to get there. The goal is to get there, make an impact, and keep growing and be allowed to grow. And I don't see that happening."

POSTGAME

The first voice heard on the air when WFAN launched in 1987 received the ultimate recognition twenty-five years later when Suzyn Waldman was inducted into the Radio Hall of Fame in the summer of 2022.

"We applaud the well-deserved recognition, particularly for Suzyn's trailblazing leadership that has been an example to so many fans and women working in our game," the MLB said in a statement.

Suzyn told me she credits her intense drive and passion to her grandfather, who told her she was a princess, and her mother, who would say, "Now that's wonderful, dear, you could do that better." She's now an inspiration to the little Suzyns in New York and around the country and even up-and-comers chasing the big leagues.

"There are five or six young women now that are down in the minor leagues, and almost all of them have said to me, 'You know, when I was a little girl, I was riding in the car with my parents, and they were listening to a Yankee game. And there you were, so I never thought I couldn't do this,' because I was there."

This applies to announcers, reporters, and female technicians in television trucks. Suzyn Waldman has proven baseball can indeed be a dream for girls.

3

Scott Spiezio

PREGAME

My son Mason and I pulled into the long, winding driveway in Morris, Illinois, in early January 2022. The former big-league ballplayer showed us around his house and the facility where he coaches local kids and shares life lessons that are more significant than he could've imagined during his playing days.

Scott Spiezio was one of the good guys. There are many like him on every MLB team I've covered—down-to-earth, normal people you look forward to chatting with throughout a baseball season. Normal, at least, on the surface. I covered Spiezio's final two years in the majors. He possessed the build of a ballplayer but the markings of a rock star. A red-dyed soul patch hung over his chin and a provocative tattoo of his then-wife, a model, covered his arm. Spiezio was living not one but two dreams: two-time world champion on the baseball diamond and lead singer of a metal band named SandFrog. Both were products of hard work, with countless swinging and singing in the house and garage we visited after a family trip to Chicago.

Mason last saw Spiezio in Florida at spring training when I covered the St. Louis Cardinals in 2007. I remember Spiezio offering to babysit four-year-old Mason and my one-year-old daughter, Ellie, so my wife and I could enjoy a night out on the town. I can't remember if I declined because I didn't want to burden a big-league ballplayer with babysitting duties or if I worried about the wild-child reputation of this good-guy athlete. Quite a bit changed over the ensuing sixteen years since I last saw Spiezio. After touring his house and baseball facility, Spiezio took us to a burger place in town for lunch. The same good guy existed, minus the soul patch and model tattoo. Plus a few extra pounds. Like Spiezio, I had just turned fifty, so I could relate to the last part.

GAME

Six months after dining with Spiezio at Honest Abe's Tap and Grill in Morris, I welcomed him as a guest on my podcast. A guy who had been to hell and back still oozed with positivity.

"Thanks for having me on. Thanks for the intro. It's a beautiful day outside and I'm looking forward to going to teach some kids some baseball and meet some new kids today and speaking with you," Spiezio said.

Spiezio grew up in Morris with one dream: to play in the big leagues. He remembers his third-grade teacher saying he needed a backup plan for baseball, but telling that to the son of a big leaguer fell on deaf ears.

"No backups. It was do-or-die for me," he recalled with laughter. Ed Spiezio suited up for the St. Louis Cardinals, San Diego Padres, and Chicago White Sox between 1964 and 1972. Scott was born six days before Ed's final MLB game in September 1972. The husband and father of three had opened a furniture store in Morris to supplement his low baseball salary. Playing the final year of his career an hour's drive from home for the Chicago White Sox meant waking up to open the store at seven, working into the afternoon before heading to Comiskey Park to play third base for the Southsiders. Ed decided to hang up his cleats to focus on family and furniture.

The older Spiezio taught Scott to switch hit at three years old and showed him the ropes at every position but catcher, eventually making him a versatile player who was drafted by the Oakland A's in the sixth round of the 1993 draft.

Scott followed in his old man's footsteps to the University of Illinois and, like his dad, became a two-time World Champion: Ed with the Cardinals and Scott with the Angels and Cardinals. He remembered what legends like Lou Brock and Bob Gibson told him when he went to Cardinals reunions with his dad as a youngster: It's easier to get to the big leagues than to stay. So, he prayed for longevity.

"'Keep me healthy. Keep everybody healthy. Let me get to the big leagues and stay ten years.' I always say I should have prayed for twenty because I got twelve."

It's what happened after twelve years that changed his life. A life on the fast track involving instant stardom eventually fell off the rails as quickly as he ascended the apex. How could it go so wrong? Who could've known as he circled the bases on October 26, 2002, in game six of the World Series?

Ed prepared Scott for the biggest stage growing up. They visualized the moment in the backyard.

"We always finished with three-two counts, two outs, bases loaded, down one, bottom of the ninth, game seven in the World Series. What are you going to do?" Spiezio recalled.

An inexperienced 2002 Angels team included Spiezio, who felt at ease, as if he had been in that moment before. Anaheim trailed the San

Francisco Giants three games to two in the World Series and faced a score of 5-0 in the bottom of the seventh. A loss would end the season and crown the Giants champions. A pair of one-out singles brought Spiezio to the plate in front of a nervous crowd of more than 44,000 Angels fans, including fifty family members and friends Spiezio flew in and bought tickets to attend.

Television analyst Tim McCarver issued a piece of cautionary advice regarding Giants reliever Félix Rodríguez: "The one area Rodríguez does not want to throw Spiezio in is that ball down and in."

The righthander kept throwing away. Spiezio fouled off pitch after pitch and eventually worked the count full in front of the electric crowd. Three balls, two strikes, and a pitch down and in. Spiezio deposited the ball over the right field wall as pandemonium broke out, and the fans erupted. Spiezio sparked the comeback and the Angels scored three more in the eighth to win and force a game seven, where they won the World Series. Angels fans will forever consider Spiezio a hero and a major piece to the franchise's only championship.

Spiezio followed with another good season with the Angels in 2003, giving him his two most productive years as a big leaguer. But the team moved in another direction in 2004, so he signed a deal with Seattle. Excited about living in a city with a music scene known for some of his favorite bands like Nirvana, Alice in Chains, Soundgarden, and Pearl Jam, Spiezio was ready to strike a chord with the Mariners. Never formally trained in music, Spiezio had bought a guitar his rookie year and started playing and writing music. Life on the road usually involved a heavy dose of music and Bible study in his room, intertwining his love of music and faith to avoid the temptations of life on the road.

"I'd seen teammates suffer through divorce and other things and addiction and alcoholism. And so it was almost like I was warning myself. It's too bad I didn't heed the warning," Spiezio told me.

A serious back injury late in spring training threatened his career, but Spiezio pressed forward, determined to heal and play, regardless of the bleak prognosis. He traveled with the team to do his rehab on the road, but without the responsibility of playing, the thirty-one-year-old wandered off track, creating habits that would change his future in the worst of ways.

"I didn't drink much at all my whole life. I didn't take an aspirin. I didn't take a Tylenol. I was the guy who was pretty much straight as an arrow. I went and talked to schools about the DARE program. I'd never seen a drug even though I had been backstage with a lot of bands . . . They all respected me and probably knew that I was innocent," Spiezio recalled.

The guy who would drink an occasional beer to fit in with teammates, even if he didn't like the taste, suddenly started drinking hard alcohol, and he liked it. Late-night excursions with no need to prepare for a game meant less Bible time and more bar time. The early stages of a downward spiral began.

"I just started making stupid decision after stupid decision, ended up having an affair which cost me my marriage," Spiezio said. He coped with the guilt and shame of disappointing his loved ones by drinking more. He played in 112 games for Seattle in 2004 and just twenty-nine in 2005 before being released by the Mariners during the summer for being "pretty much useless," in his words.

By November, sure that his playing days had ended, he continued the heavy drinking and tried cocaine for the first time. Unaware of his personal struggles, the St. Louis Cardinals offered Spiezio an invite to spring training camp, and he made the team. He admits he still drank too much but found a refocused energy playing for a historic franchise, his father's old organization. He even hit two home runs in a game in September, leading the Cardinals to a win in Arizona. The lines of cocaine he did the night before must have given him some luck, he thought, so he justified using it occasionally. Baseball is a sport of superstitions, usually involving silly quirks like not stepping on lines. Sniffing them was generally not part of the formula, but Spiezio called the season magical, and he won his second World Championship.

Life could not be better on the outside, but a look on the inside revealed disaster. The slow-rolling snowball picked up momentum in the offseason, and addiction soon ruled his life. He somehow managed to play in sixty-nine games for St. Louis from April through early August 2007, living two lives as a big-league ballplayer as well as a high-functioning alcoholic and addict.

"I could stay up all night and drink a handle of vodka and do stuff and still play at a high level," he recalled. "I felt like it was normal. But I started needing to drink in order not to shake."

He tried to hide it, but his teammates and coaches knew and eventually convinced him to check into rehab on August 10, 2007. He returned to the team five weeks later, just before his thirty-fifth birthday, and played in twelve more games to end the year. They would be the last of his career. Though Spiezio was determined to make the team in 2008, the Cardinals, who had supported him throughout his struggles, felt the need to part ways. Spiezio began what he called a "ten-year detour" that included five arrests, multiple divorces, the loss of almost all of his career earnings, and most importantly, an erosion of the relationships with his parents and his children, not to mention declining health. Some details remain cloudy or even forgotten due to periods of blacking out. Spending thousands of dollars a week on cocaine and consuming gallons of vodka will do that. He missed games and graduations. His oldest son, Cody, started addressing him as Scott because he didn't want to call him Dad anymore. His youngest son, Tyler, wondered why he couldn't have a normal father.

His daughter changed her last name to honor her stepfather and his positive influence on her life.

Spiezio estimates he went to rehab eleven times over the next decade. Always an upbeat optimist, he maintained his faith and a belief he could shake his disease.

"I figured each time that I went, I had a better chance of succeeding. Each time I went, I thought it was gonna be the last time, but I kept falling."

The problem was, he could never get past the first step of Alcoholics Anonymous and admitting to being powerless over alcohol and life becoming unmanageable.

"I thought, *I'm different. I'm not powerless over anything.* And, of course, I finally figured I was wrong."

3,840 days after playing his last MLB game, Spiezio began a new chapter of sobriety, taking his last drink on April 5, 2018. He says giving up drugs and alcohol is the hardest thing he's done in his life. The reward is a rebuilt relationship with his parents, family, and friends. He vows to his daughter and two sons every year on his sobriety anniversary to take care of them and never go back to the partying lifestyle. Former championship teammates from the Angels and Cardinals sent videos to celebrate five years without drinking in 2023.

He's a believer in second chances. "If you kind of lose yourself, go back to your hometown, find those true friends, find those roots, and they'll help you find yourself again, and that's what happened with me."

POSTGAME

June 10, 2023, marked another milestone and memorable moment, one worth celebrating, as Spiezio spoke in front of fans at Christian Day after a St. Louis Cardinals game. Ed Spiezio, the proud father who was so heartbroken with his son's decline in 2006 that he could not watch the World Series, was in attendance all these years later to watch Scott's testimony at Busch Stadium. "He gave me a hug, and he was crying and told me how proud he was of me."

Spiezio spends regular time reading the Bible, attending church, helping addicts, and teaching kids the finer points of baseball and life in Morris. He's trying to make an impact on anyone's life he can touch. So when I asked him, "What's the biggest home run you've hit in your life?" as I asked every one of my podcast guests, he pivoted to something much more important than any home run on or off the field.

"I can help to save people's lives now with the things that I've been through. And so that's probably the biggest joy when I see people changing in their lives: that I've gotten a chance to be a part of that." His message to kids in schools is simple: Don't try it even once. The risk of fentanyl and sudden death far outweighs any instant gratification.

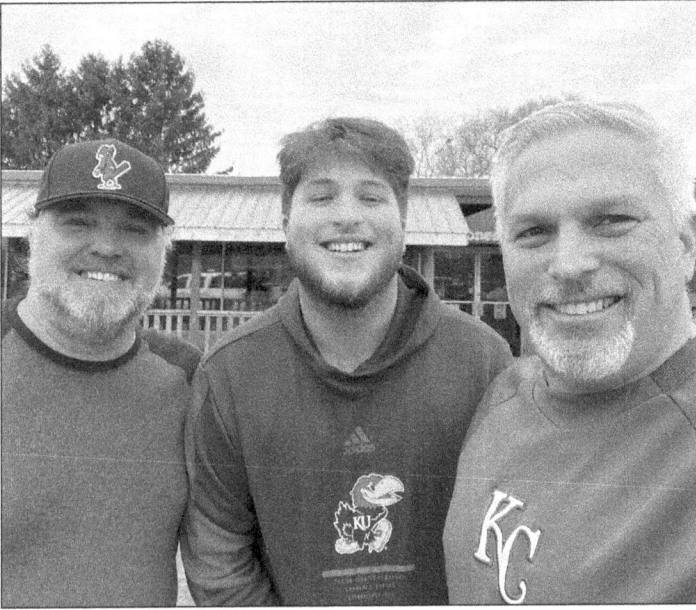

His message to anyone struggling is one of inspiration, molded by his own experiences: "As long as you have a breath, you've got a pen to write a great ending, and it's never too late to start getting better and mending relationships and getting healthy."

4

Sarah Nauser

PREGAME

The crowd gathered on a picture-perfect late afternoon on May 29, 2021.

"Family and friends, thank you all for coming today to share in this wonderful occasion. Today, we are here together to unite Sarah and Lonnie in marriage."

I'm not sure if the couple ever dreamt of a wedding quite like this. A quick yet deeply meaningful ceremony wrapped up in front of a picturesque pond as guests wrestled with their emotions.

"Sarah and Lonnie have chosen rings to exchange with each other as a symbol of their unending love. Lonnie, as you place this ring on Sarah's finger, please repeat after me. With this ring, I thee wed and pledge you my love now and forever. Sarah, as you place this ring on Lonnie's finger, please repeat after me. With this ring, I thee wed and pledge you my love now and forever."

What would "forever" mean? How many years? I'm sure others had to wonder. The thought crossed my mind as I made one final statement.

"By the authority vested in me by the State of Missouri, I now pronounce you husband and wife."

GAME

Sarah Nauser is the only person highlighted in these pages who was also featured in my first book, *Small Ball Big Results*. I'm writing about her again because describing her battle with amyotrophic lateral sclerosis, or ALS, and her upbeat outlook could not possibly have been the final chapter I wrote about her. The doctors may have predicted the end of her life, but they drastically missed the timeline.

I first met Sarah when she appeared on our pregame show at Kauffman Stadium in August 2018. The twenty-nine-year-old police officer with the radiant smile masking the disease that would soon be impossible to hide. Still able to walk mostly on her own, she made the first of many appearances on *Royals Live* and became a friend and inspiration to current and former baseball players from her favorite team, the Kansas City Royals. The "Positivity" chapter in my first book ended with Sarah's optimism as she prepared for her upcoming wedding in May 2021. She felt so fortunate that George Brett, the greatest Royal of all time, would officiate her wedding. Telling the next stage of Sarah's story feels like the most miraculous bonus because the doctors told her she wouldn't make it this long. Our friendship evolved, and Sarah became someone my wife, son, and daughter would consider family. She even asked me to officiate her wedding when a conflict arose for Brett.

I've watched Sarah lose the ability to walk and use her hands, yet her mind is sharp, and I believe she's mentally stronger than ever. We've regularly texted late at night about the Royals over the years. Here's a confession I've never told Sarah: I usually shy away from talking about baseball after I leave the stadium. Conversations with friends can often go to a negative place, and I refuse to let losing streaks bring me down. Complaining when your team is struggling is part of being a fan, but my ability to separate myself from the cynicism allows me to maintain my energy every day at work. Talking baseball with Sarah (or I should say "texting" for me and "texting with her eyes" for her) always feels right. Her positive outlook and personal connection to all the Royals players make every exchange fun. Plus, selfishly, I know I'm guaranteed to go to sleep hopeful and inspired by our conversations. Almost every text thread with Sarah begins or ends with words that can't seem possible from someone living with ALS: "It was a great day," or some version of that.

Positivity has remained a constant in Sarah's life, as well as three other P words, which are small ball traits and keys to dreamers: Perspective, Persistence, and Purpose. It's easy to feel sorry for someone going through a hellish nightmare of a disease like ALS, and by no means do I lack empathy for Sarah. But her constant ability to find perspective rarely allows time for moments of sorrow. Since her diagnosis, she has checked off bucket list items at a frantic pace. Some are fun and cool, others personal, and all are meaningful. Trips with Lonnie and each of her siblings have allowed Sarah to enjoy life to the fullest. Even with limited mobility, she basked in the sunshine of St. Thomas and took in the majestic views while floating in the water for hours. The discovery of a beach wheelchair unlocked a freedom she didn't think possible.

"I was able to find normalcy in a sense even though I didn't have the physical strength. I was able to do everything everyone else was doing," she told me.

A long flight to China in early 2020, just as COVID-19 broke out, enabled Sarah to stay in a medical clinic for two weeks. She received three spinal injections of mesenchymal stem cells as well as daily infusions designed to clean toxins from her body. She grew stronger and even regained the ability to feed herself. The treatment, not available in the United States, is believed to be most effective every six months but COVID-19 prevented her from continuing. She does believe the treatment slowed down the progression of ALS significantly.

After Sarah's diagnosis, she watched the movie Gleason about former pro football player Steve Gleason. Gleason began his battle with ALS in 2011, and Sarah found inspiration from the one-time Indianapolis Colt and New Orleans Saint, who was still fighting in 2021 when she visited the Crescent City to see the man whose inspirational footsteps she would follow.

"I realized living with this disease was not only possible but could still be amazing. I was able to have a conversation with Steve even though he can no longer speak. I witnessed him using eye gaze technology to not only converse with me but also with players who came over to say hi. It eased a lot of my fears and worries about the disease and what could potentially happen in my future as the disease progressed."

Sarah's hero growing up was her older brother, Kurtis. She gladly walked in his shadow but years later the role model began to fade as Kurtis struggled with drug addiction. After her diagnosis with ALS, Sarah saw tears in Kurtis's eyes as she broke the devastating news to him. The siblings supported each other going forward as she navigated the sudden change of life, and he rode the roller coaster of ups and downs that often accompany addiction. From rock bottom to rehab, Kurtis could count on constant support from his baby sister.

"We motivated each other. I was slowly getting my hero back," she wrote in one of her countless heartwarming posts on social media.

As he became sober, the two discussed Sarah's dream of visiting ballparks. They fulfilled another long-held aspiration of Sarah's by attending a game at Wrigley Field in Chicago in August 2021.

"Dreams do come true," she wrote. "We were able to see Wrigley Field together. Even more special, I got my big brother back. He's been sober over two years and is my biggest fan."

I wrote in my first book that numerous players and the Kansas City Royals manager Ned Yost became invested in Sarah's story largely because of her beaming smile and infectious personality. Her first spring training trip in 2019 remained vivid in her memories years later. Sarah quickly realized that the Royals viewed her as family. One of her childhood idols, former Royals captain Mike Sweeney, drove her in a golf cart to center field and prayed with her.

"A powerful moment I will treasure forever," she told me. "I had the support of my favorite sports team with me as I fought my fight. It lifted me up then and still does today," she proudly said.

By the end of the 2022 season, most of the names and faces she knew had retired or moved on to new teams. Yet here she was in late February of 2023, making a trip to Surprise, Arizona, to take in some spring training action. I had just missed Sarah and Lonnie, flying home after finishing interviews and a game assignment a day before they arrived. When I looked on social media and saw a picture the next day, I had to send her a message that simply read, "Greatest picture ever." Sarah was in her wheelchair at home plate, surrounded by more than two dozen players and coaches.

"I don't think I could have possibly dreamt of a better day," she texted me. "It was so special! The guys were so excited to meet me. I was blown away. I didn't know what to expect not having met so many of them but they were so awesome. It was unreal. I got in the van and happy tears flowed. I said, 'How did I possibly get so lucky?' Days like this ignite that fire to fight harder than ever."

The 2023 baseball season for the Royals often involved players taking the field with t-shirts featuring one word on the back: *PERSISTENT*. The front of the blue shirt had the caricature of a blond woman—Sarah—flexing her muscles. The words *FIGHT LIKE A GIRL, FIGHT TO CURE ALS, #SARAHSSOLDIERS* were written in a circle around the image. She watches Royals baseball every night unless she's attending a game with Lonnie. How do I know this? Any shoutout I've ever given her results in a text message to me in a matter of seconds. One time, it was how I found out I had lost my red Sarah's Soldiers bracelet I had worn for years. During the first commercial of our show, a text came in.

"Where is your bracelet?"

It had come off earlier in the day, caught in a long-sleeve shirt I had changed out of. I had no idea until she messaged. And she always sees when the players are wearing her shirt in an interview.

"I am so damn happy. It is so cool they support me the way they do."

I receive some version of that message every time she spots it.

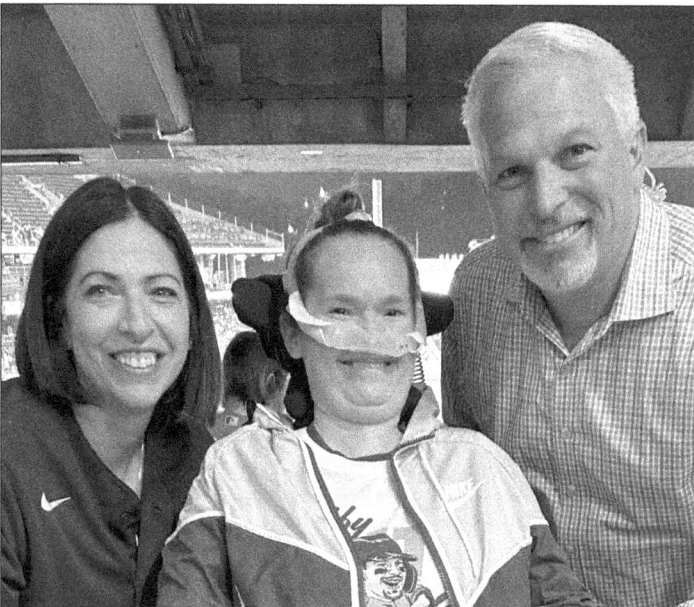

Here's the thing—she supports them too. It's not uncommon for a player to hear from Sarah during a slump or after an injury with an inspirational message. Michael Massey, a down-to-earth, thoughtful second baseman for Kansas City, regularly messages with Sarah.

"She's just genuine. There are not many people outside of your family and maybe some close friends that actually get happy when you do well and feel it when you don't," Massey told me in one of our many conversations about Sarah.

I sent her a video from the visiting clubhouse at Guaranteed Rate Field in Chicago on her thirty-fifth birthday in September 2023. I would never record a personal video inside the locker room, because I feel it violates the players' personal space. But I knew for Sarah, I could pull it off, with the help of Royals superstar and captain Salvador Perez.

"Hey Sarah, I'm in the Royals clubhouse with maybe your favorite person. I'm not your favorite; this guy is," as I panned over to Salvy, who said in his Venezuelan accent while flashing a peace sign, "Sarah, wishing you the best. Happy birthday. Hey, follow me." I proceeded to follow Salvy, who elicited Happy Birthday and *Feliz Cumpleaños* greetings from Americans, Venezuelans, Cubans, and anyone else in the room.

When one of her favorite players is traded or signs with a new team, she immediately texts me in anguish, but I remind her about the opportunity to grow Sarah's Soldiers nationwide. Former Royal Ryan O'Hearn, a favorite of Sarah's, continued to stay in touch with her after becoming a Baltimore Oriole. I interviewed Sarah in June 2023 on MLB's Lou Gehrig Day for our *Royals Live* pregame show, a miracle considering doctors didn't expect her to live that long, let alone be able to physically talk. Wearing the "Fights Like a Girl" t-shirt with her likeness on it and some blue Air Jordans to match her team's color, she spoke into the microphone eloquently once again.

"Honestly, I didn't ever know if I would get to see today so the fact that I still have my voice and I'm still here to make a difference means everything to me."

The interview was posted on social media, and O'Hearn, in the middle of a season with the Orioles, responded, "I just watched your interview with Joel and it brought me to tears. So honored to call you a friend. You inspire me to be as badass as you are!"

She texted me a screenshot and said, "How cool is this?" All I could do was agree.

O'Hearn, one of my favorite people in the game, explained it to me: "Every time I see Sarah, she has such a positive outlook . . . I don't know if anyone could go through something like [ALS] with more grace. It's an honor to know her and be a small part of her journey."

I remind her all the time about her effect on others. She knows, but she still can't believe it.

"I never imagined I could have such an impact and inspire all kinds. It really blows my mind."

POSTGAME

Five years after her diagnosis, I told Sarah I believe she's found a deeper purpose in life than her personal battle. She agreed and put her eyes to work to send me these powerful words.

"I think my greatest purpose is being a light in this world. Lifting up others. Showing others that regardless of the battle you are up against, you can not only defy the odds but also enjoy the little things in life as you do. Everyone sees the fight I am up against, from the breathing machine to the wheelchair, but even greater than that, they see the constant smile on my face, and they can't help but smile themselves. At first, I just wanted to make a positive impact on ALS and those battling the disease, but because of my transparency and willingness to share my feelings and thoughts about life, my reach has gone further than I could have imagined. All I ever wanted to do with my life was to help others, which is why I made the choice to be a police officer. But now I have a voice or a mindset capable of helping people from all over the world. One of my favorite quotes, even long before ALS, is, 'A life is not important except in the impact it has on other lives.'"

I've talked so many times on television about Jackie Robinson and Lou Gehrig. Two baseball legends I never met, yet their spirit, fight, and impact live on through my friend Sarah Nauser.

5

Peter Mallouk

PREGAME

Former first baseman Will Clark stood on the field holding court during batting practice at Oracle Park, one of the nicest stadiums in all of baseball, situated on the San Francisco Bay. Always an entertaining and animated storyteller, Clark, a six-time All-Star, mostly with the Giants in the 1980s and '90s, talked about old times with an attentive audience of Kansas City broadcasters before a Royals-Giants game in April 2023.

I first met Clark in the summer of 2000, my second full season covering the St. Louis Cardinals as a reporter for the local Fox television affiliate. Baltimore traded the thirty-six-year-old to the Cards to replace injured slugger Mark McGwire, and I braced for the challenge that might lie ahead of interviewing an intimidating veteran. Clark featured one of the sweetest left-handed swings in the game, and an intensity and scowl that could scare opposing pitchers (and young reporters). To my surprise, I found the Mississippi native, who would soon retire, to be one of the more engaging players in the game. I interviewed him live in Atlanta after the Cardinals swept the Braves in the playoffs. Champagne was flying across the visiting clubhouse at Turner Field, but Clark celebrated with two other beverages, proudly pouring beer from one hand and a bottle of

Jack Daniels from the other. I knew when we saw him on the field with the Giants, serving in an advisory role he held with the ball club twenty-three seasons later, his anecdotes would be just as entertaining, but it was actually a story from my broadcast colleague Ryan Lefebvre that left us all laughing hysterically.

Ryan grew up in a baseball household, the son of former MLB player and manager Jim Lefebvre. His childhood included meeting superstars like Pete Rose, Nolan Ryan, Willie Stargell, Dave Parker, Mike Schmidt, and in the summer of 1986, Will Clark. Clark joined the Giants AAA minor league affiliate in Phoenix during an injury rehab assignment at a time when major league clubhouses always provided copies of *USA Today*'s detailed sports section well before the internet existed. Clark wanted to read the publication, but a minor league locker room rarely featured the same amenities provided in the majors, so he summoned the teenage bat boy. He handed him a ten-dollar bill, tossed him car keys, and asked him to go find a *USA Today* at the gas station.

He either didn't realize the boy was the manager's son or didn't care but when Ryan informed Clark, "I'm only fifteen years old," the fiery first baseman shot back, "I didn't ask you how old you were. I asked you to get me a *USA Today*," as a room full of players all observed the conversation. It's almost certain that an expletive fit somewhere in that sentence. Ryan clearly remembers Clark telling him to keep the change, and so after obtaining the paper, he paid the Taco Bell drive-thru a visit before returning to the stadium with the newspaper and a bag of tacos.

As he recalled the details, Clark, now fifty-nine years old, laughed. I found myself thinking of a recent story I heard from one of the most successful business leaders to appear on my podcast.

GAME

Well before Peter Mallouk became the CEO of a top national wealth advisory firm in the United States, a *New York Times* best-selling author, and a highly sought-after thought leader and speaker, he worked in the visiting clubhouse as a teenager at Kauffman Stadium, or Royals Stadium as it was called in the 1980s. He vividly remembers Wade Boggs, one of the best hitters of his generation and a future MLB Hall of Famer, asking for chicken. Baseball history includes endless tales of superstitious players, and Boggs, a twelve-time All-Star on the field, can head up an All-Star team of the most superstitious.

"I probably had in the neighborhood of seventy-five to eighty superstitions that I had to go through during the course of the day" Boggs said on the radio show *Legends Lounge* on SiriusXM. His ritual included anything from taking batting practice and running sprints at the same time to eating so much chicken before a game that some teammates referred to him as "Chicken Man." With the frequency of Boggs' success at the plate, why would he tweak any of his odd habits? Hitting streaks were as much a part of his routine as the superstitions, and he found himself in another hot stretch during a visit to Kansas City one season. Unfortunately, the visiting locker room had no chicken before a Red Sox–Royals game, so the clubhouse manager gave Peter, who *did* have a license, his keys. The mission was simple for the teenager: don't put Boggs in a "fowl" mood.

"There's no GPS, there are no cell phones, I have no idea where I'm going, and I'm driving around, and I run out of gas. I have to wait until some police show up. And it was literally one of the worst days of my life," Mallouk recalled.

He returned to the stadium sure his poultry plight would end Boggs' streak, with the hitter's pregame meal altered.

Peter nervously watched every at-bat. "I just held my breath the whole game, [thinking] that I was gonna get fired."

Thankfully, Boggs managed a hit, taking the young clubbie off the hook.

Ballplayers who make it to "The Show" should be considered an outlier in the world of sports. Anyone who plays even one MLB game has overcome the most impossible odds. Boggs represented an even smaller percentage of ultimate success stories. The same could be said about Peter Mallouk, his family, and his career path.

So how does someone become so financially successful that he can buy a piece of the same MLB team he once worked for as a teenager? Clients, friends, and strangers ask Mallouk for advice on how to get rich every day, but the secret sauce may not open eyes for its originality. It stands the test of time, however, in any profession, and was passed down to me by my parents as well, who had no background in the broadcasting industry but preached the importance of hard work.

"You're living in a place and a time where if you can just out-hustle somebody else, outwork somebody else, it really is enough. There are so many people trying to shortcut the system," Mallouk told me.

Yes, you need talent. I'm pretty sure most of us can work on hitting a fastball every day and still not make the big leagues. Shooting hundreds of jump shots with NBA expectations? Being 6'10" would help and we cannot control our height. Or as Mallouk recognizes regarding life, "There is a lottery that takes place. My luck started before I was born."

Peter painted a picture of life in Egypt for his parents before he existed in 1969. After finishing medical school, his father, Alex, received a job offer to practice in Uganda but wanted to follow his siblings to a different location. Many of Alex's eight brothers and sisters left Egypt to live in Canada and Europe, so Alex and his wife chose to follow his family, and they paid a visit to the Canadian Embassy in Egypt. A long line on this day prevented them from completing paperwork before the office closed, so they left. They passed the US Embassy on their walk home and noticed it was open with no line. American officials told the Mallouks that access to the US was limited to doctors, teachers, and engineers. Good thing, because Mr. and Mrs. Mallouk were a doctor and teacher.

"Less than thirty days later, they were in the United States in a German family's basement with the classic couple hundred dollars [in their pocket] . . . .Now, if that story doesn't happen, you know, I don't have anything," Peter said more than fifty years later.

Born ten months after the move to the US, Peter recognized the luck involved. "I'm pretty sure the Creative Planning story does not happen in Uganda."

Peter grew up like many American kids, wanting to be an astronaut or athlete, but caught the entrepreneurial bug at a young age and saw a more realistic and attainable path to success.

"This idea of looking at a marketplace and saying, 'How do I do something better or faster or with more value than somebody else?' And have the market tell you if you're right or wrong; that has always been the one thing that's always appealed to me."

After graduating from the University of Kansas, Mallouk earned an MBA and a law degree from KU. He began working at Creative Planning in 1998 and became the wealth management company's president and CEO in 2004. Along the way, he built the company, earned numerous accolades, became a regular expert on national television shows, a featured speaker with Tony Robbins, and one of the top philanthropists in Kansas City, along with his wife, Veronica. Beyond the hard work, what's the key to running a highly successful national wealth management company?

"I think that culture is like a cake," Mallouk told me. "You can't just put five ingredients together. There is an art to it, too. And you can't be missing one ingredient, even if it's a tiny, tiny, tiny ingredient. And the things that we care about at Creative Planning, not everybody cares about."

Culture can only become successful with the right people who believe in that culture. Growth and scaling often challenge an organization in maintaining its culture but Mallouk believes the Creative Planning culture has provided a blueprint.

"It's gotten easier because we have more people to choose from. And we've gotten better at figuring out what works and doesn't work," Mallouk said.

Staying true to the people and culture instead of looking for shortcuts has been the formula.

"Every single person that walks through that door can make the place better, or they can make it a heck of a lot worse. So it's by far the biggest decision we make day to day."

Hard work, culture, and the right people make all the difference, but how does a relatively well-known entity in the smaller independent world manage to swim in the bigger sea with the likes of Merrill Lynch and Morgan Stanley? First and foremost is a message I hear often in baseball and sports. Keep it simple. Mallouk understood that being a consistent hitter like Wade Boggs in the finance world meant communicating with clients in a way that empowered them.

"I really thought about trying to come up with a process that appealed to my dad, who's an internist, and my mom as a teacher. And so if they could understand it and enjoy it, anyone would, because they're just not interested in finance at all. That was probably aha moment number one."

Keep it simple and stay true during tough times.

Aha moments number two and three came during the 2008 financial crisis and the COVID-19 pandemic in 2020. Creative Planning emerged stronger following each disastrous period.

"We've been intentional only about one thing, which is, how can we make what we're doing more valuable for the client? How can we solve more of their problems? How can we create more alignment with them and be better than everyone else that we see in the marketplace."

The other expression I hear every day in baseball is "control the controllable." Pitchers can't control whether a fielder makes a play or not. Hitters can't control scalding a ball with hard contact, only to have the outfielder rob a home run by reaching over the wall. The good ones stick to what works every time. Creative did the same during 2008–2009 and in 2020, and clients noticed.

Mallouk loves to tell the story of legendary rock band Van Halen and their original lead singer, David Lee Roth, who made absurd demands at concert venues that often included specific instructions about what M&M's to include or exclude in the green room. Mallouk, a huge music fan, heard an interview with Roth years after he left Van Halen, where he admitted having no interest in anyone separating M&M's to satisfy his perceived prima donna ways. The contractual demands were really meant to test the venue's ability to pay attention to details. Would they read the contract? If so, the odds of a safer concert amidst pyrotechnics were more likely. Mallouk feels like the pandemic provided similar moments.

"People are too busy to really pay attention to anything, or they're just too busy. And so you get their hyperattention briefly. And those are your chances, when you've got that hyperattention, to really prove yourself to them." Mallouk tapped into his old baseball clubhouse years to make an analogy. "It's like a sports team. We're really set up where there's these subcultures. There's the tax group and the legal group and the trust group.

But what makes them great is the way they can come together to make that play happen right at the end of the game. And I think that they did that. In a way, we wouldn't have had the opportunity without the pandemic to really show what the firm was capable of. And I think that we gave those clients that chance to see those separated M&M's and gave them the clue that we're able to do what we've told you we're gonna be able to do."

POSTGAME

Peter Mallouk's life came full circle in late 2019. At least full circle from the fifteen-year-old boy who showed up at Royals Stadium in the 1980s. Back then, he wanted to work for his favorite team, so his father drove him to the ballpark. He had no inside connections to the team, just an avid fan who learned an early lesson in seeking out a cool job. "If you don't ask, you're not going to get." The clubhouse job allowed him to rub elbows with Wade Boggs and the biggest stars in the game. Fast forward to 2019, when Kansas City businessman John Sherman was searching for a group of investors to ultimately buy the Royals. Mallouk, the extremely successful, humble, and philanthropic entrepreneur known for his calm and deliberate decision-making, was presented with a thirty-slide PowerPoint about the organization he so loved as a boy. Before the first slide ended, Mallouk shouted out, "I'm done. I'm in. I want to do this . . . I'm good. I am ready to go."

The kid born down the road to Egyptian immigrants, who had built a life-changing wealth management company, would now own a piece of the Royals.

"To go from shining shoes at the visitor's clubhouse to being able to be in the owner's box. I feel like I'm a spectator and imposter. But I'm loving every minute of it."

6

Ted Barrett

PREGAME

October 21, 2014, brought palpable anticipation to Kauffman Stadium as eager fans poured through the turnstiles. A loyal but previously hopeless fanbase nervously awaited its team's first appearance in the World Series in twenty-nine years, hours before the home plate umpire would yell, "Play ball!" No one noticed the six men sharply dressed in suits, who looked more like agents or lawyers, walking around the field. I knew all six men, including their crew chief, Jeff Kellogg. Just like players, managers, and coaches, umpires are part of the people I'm fortunate enough to know in the game of baseball.

I first met Kellogg in 2011, when I decided to follow him, along with his crew, on a visit to Kansas City's Children's Mercy Hospital. He, Tim Timmons, Eric Cooper, and Mark Carlson were going to spend time with sick children and hand out teddy bears while staying in town to work a Royals series. I thought showing another side of the game's officials could be interesting.

"Putting a smile on a kids' face is the easiest call of all," Timmons told me as part of a feature that ran on our pregame show.

I walked down to their locker room before that evening's game to thank them for their time and they encouraged me to come visit the locker room whenever they had the Royals on their schedule. Over the years, as they split up and worked with other umpiring crews, I would knock on the locker room door any time any of the four was in the same stadium and eventually got to know every umpire in the league, including one of the best in the business, Ted Barrett.

As Kellogg, Cooper, and the crew took pictures at home plate to mark the honor of working baseball's most significant event, Barrett stood out above the rest, in part because of his 6'2", 255-pound frame, not to mention his dapper suit and topcoat. The man known as "Reverend" had a way of bringing people together.

GAME

Young Ted "Teddy" Barrett, or Edward when his mother's tone became stern, hailed from near Buffalo, New York. He dreamed of NFL glory and heavyweight boxing titles. Umpiring Major League Baseball's World Series never found its way into Teddy's dreams, although he did work a little league game for the first time with a friend at fourteen and grew to enjoy being in the middle of the action. Still, a career enforcing the law of the game seemed far-fetched for a boy who usually found himself complaining to officials about their calls in all sports. Eventually, he began to appreciate the underappreciated.

"Once I started doing it, I was like, whoa, this is really hard. I'm not going to yell at an umpire anymore."

His athletic abilities remained a priority, leading him to play football at Cal State Hayward. As he racked up mileage on his car to visit his girlfriend (now wife), Ted's dad suggested he find a job to pay for gas and insurance. Not wanting to follow his friends into fast food and appliance store types of vocations, he chose to umpire three to four high school baseball games a week. At fifty dollars a pop in the 1980s, Teddy felt good about his earning power.

"I was flush with cash. And so that really started me thinking, man, I'd like to do more of this," he told me.

After his playing career ended, he wanted to coach football and supplement his income by umpiring college baseball. Barrett moved to Las Vegas after college and tapped into his boxing abilities, working out as a sparring partner with some elite stars, including world champions with names like Mike Tyson and George Foreman. He said he remembers the beatings from Foreman the most.

"I tell people he hit me so hard that my son was born two years later with a headache . . . He was just like a tank coming at you, but of course, Mike Tyson was just so fast and strong."

Marriage awaited, and taking knockout blows quickly grew old. His father offered to pay for five weeks of umpire training.

"My goal really was to go five weeks at umpire school, and then maybe it would help me down the road with (umpiring) college ball . . . It was great not getting punched out in the Florida sun."

He traded in getting punched for punching hitters out with strikeouts at the plate and soon received an invite to work in the minor leagues.

Umpiring pro games may have represented a huge opportunity, but the salary at the lowest levels of spring training paled in comparison to his prior fifty-dollars-per-game moonlighting gig. Teddy worked on a two-man crew and was essentially attached to his work partner on and off the field as they struggled to survive financially. The duo was paid nineteen dollars a day working in Arizona, and they split a hotel, rotating weekly between the bed and the couch. A daily rent of eleven dollars meant they lived off of eight bucks a day.

"We got creative. We would go to happy hour buffets and buy the cheapest thing we could just to eat, but we were having fun. We were professional umpires."

As Barrett rose, working in the Texas League at the AA level of minor league ball, the pay increased modestly, but taking care of his wife and two young children became his most significant priority. He had a version of a conversation I think everyone with a family who works in sports has with their spouses at some point, including me.

"If it ever gets to that point where you want me to come home, I give you permission to do that," he told his wife, "but don't do it lightly because I'll come home if you ask me to."

She never did and the eventual reward of umpiring at the highest level came to fruition when Barrett made his big league debut in 1994. Only two hundred minor league umpiring jobs existed with hundreds of new candidates graduating from umpiring school annually. Major League Baseball offers about sixty spots, with most big leaguers holding positions for decades. Ted Barrett defied the odds. No longer worried about affording a hotel room, Barrett made in a day what he earned in a month as a minor leaguer. He could fly his wife and children to any city in America and bring them to World Series and All-Star Games along the way.

Had he not reached the big leagues, Barrett would have pursued the ministry, which he ultimately did, embracing a role at the pulpit while calling balls and strikes.

"When I got to the big leagues, that call didn't go away. And I thought God was calling me out to go be a missionary or go serve him somewhere. And I thought, man, this is a dirty trick. I've overcome these tremendous odds, you know, to get here, and now you're pulling me out. And he's just like, 'No, you dummy. I've put you in the big leagues for a reason. And that's to be a minister.' And so my flock was the umpires that I worked with."

A man who called fair and foul now carried a reputation that meant players trying to avoid foul language, often apologizing to The Reverend. Yet he never judged and tried to remember that the players, like umpires, are human beings.

"I'm gonna do the best I can . . . we all have bad days, and sometimes you're not on your best behavior. And I hope then there's grace and forgiveness that way. Relationships are important."

Barrett thought about that often when a struggling player might lash out in a tirade filled with colorful language.

"If a player is frustrated, he's going through a zero-for-thirty slump, and he vents his frustration on me, fans don't see a lot of times he's coming back the next day and saying, 'Hey, I'm sorry,' and same thing happens with umpires. We all go through bad performance stretches."

These are lessons to be learned from a man who enforced the rules in a game that involves failure.

"If I had a bad game, I couldn't wait for the next day to get back out there. Because there's going to be another game, and they'll forget about the game before, and I'll do my best this game, and then we'll just move on," Barrett told me, adding, "If you are locked up in fear, you're not going to do well. So you just have to free yourself of that. Know you're going to make mistakes. For me, mistakes are an opportunity to learn. And that's how I got better."

Barrett had no shortage of big moments on the diamond, working three perfect games, including two as the home plate umpire. The first took place in 1999 when David Cone retired all twenty-seven batters he faced as a star for the New York Yankees. The other featured Matt Cain for the San Francisco Giants in 2012. World Series assignments in 2011 for the St. Louis Cardinals and the Texas Rangers classic, as well as the 2014 Series featuring the Kansas City Royals and San Francisco Giants, provided endless drama, with both matchups going a full seven games. Like an athlete locked into the zone, most umpires fail to fully grasp the moment until later reflection.

"You're just staying clinical, you're staying locked in. And so even as we walk off the field, it takes a while to kind of decompress and get away from that. And then you can look back and go, 'Wow, that was really cool,'" Barrett told me.

The manager of the 2014 World Champion Giants was Bruce Bochy, a man who gave Barrett a piece of advice way back when the two crossed paths in rookie ball that stuck with him throughout his career.

"He pulled me aside one day. He said, 'You're not going to do well in this job because all you want to do is fight.' It took me a couple of years to really realize what he was saying. I learned that staying calm and being reasonable will go a long way," Barrett said.

It reminded me of advice I received from Royals all-time wins leader Paul Splittorff during my first year working in KC. I considered Splitt the greatest mentor for the three seasons I worked with him on TV before cancer took his life in 2011.

"There are a lot of important people who are paid a lot of money to lose sleep over the losses, and you're not one of them."

He had seen me getting frustrated with the losses and wanted me to know I had a job to do, win or lose. I learned not to let the results affect my positive energy and that I can stay even keel no matter what. That's what made Barrett so respected. His calm demeanor and skill kept him in the game.

Other life lessons learned on the diamond from the retired umpire: "When you mess up, you fess up. So when we make mistakes, instead of trying to cover those mistakes, confess it, get it out there and move on," he said, telling me there was a sermon in those words.

Like most of the world, the game has changed due to technology. When Barrett broke in, the goal was consistency. Now, 100 percent perfection is expected with the fancy cameras, angles, and resources available to players, coaches, fans, as well as the league office. It's not fully achievable, but the relationships and communication aspect of the game remain as important as ever.

"I never worked a game where I walked off the field and went, man, I was 100 percent right. I got every pitch right . . . Laying in bed at night, it's hard for Major League umpires to sleep after a game because these pitches are running through your mind. And now, the next day, we'll open up and get our performance feedback. The players, they go right back to the dugout, look at the iPad. They've got instant feedback. We have to kind of chew on it overnight."

More significant than any on-field calls were officiating countless weddings of big-league and minor-league umpires as well as funerals of umpires Wally Bell and Eric Cooper. Yes, the man who worked the 2014 World Series with Barrett, who I first met during that hospital visit, tragically passed away in 2019. I attended Cooper's funeral in Des

Moines, Iowa, after getting a call from Carlson to inform me of Cooper's devastating death after he developed blood clots. I wanted to pay respects to Cooper and all the umpires who form as strong a bond and fraternity as any group in sports. Sitting in the church listening to stories of Coop was heart wrenching, yet I found myself moved by the calmness and compassion of Barrett. The umpire served a role that day more important than any game on the field.

POSTGAME

While he never originally aspired to make it a career, Ted Barrett learned a lesson that would've helped him be successful in any field, including on a baseball field.

"A long time ago, my parents taught me in order to get respect, you gotta give respect. And I think I gave ballplayers and coaches and managers respect. And I think that was reciprocated."

Anyone can learn from Barrett's life advice. First, he says, "Dream big and then work your way to get there. But also, don't take any shortcuts . . . you've got to go out every day and never take a day off. Because you never know who's watching."

Second, "You've got to get better. And the only way you're gonna get better is by working hard."

And finally, "Sometimes you've got to look in the mirror. And you have to say, what can I do better? Am I doing my best? You know, am I getting better?"

Barrett retired after the 2022 season but continued his work as a minister to umpires and others around the game, combining his love of baseball, umpiring, and religion. Add in family and a little wind therapy, and life will be good. He can often be found on his motorcycle in Arizona with friends, riding, heading to lunch and taking part in Bible study, trading in balls and strikes for a higher calling.

1

Nancy Goldberg

PREGAME

I truly love going to work to cover baseball, even during the tough times. Friends often wonder how I'm doing when a losing streak stretches from days into weeks, but I'm still living my dream of talking about sports on television. Fighting through the mental fatigue while always remembering how fortunate I am to do what I love makes going to work a true joy.

That was not the case on July 4, 2022. I was walking around downtown Houston in the extreme heat, hoping to sweat before cleaning up and going to work for a late afternoon game at Minute Maid Park. I only remember that the Astros won on a walk-off home run by Yordan Alvarez to break a tie in the ninth inning because I looked it up while writing this book. My stronger memories include a panicked text and a complete lack of interest in talking about "America's pastime" on what is usually such a patriotic day for the United States. How could I go on the air and say, "Happy Fourth of July. There's nothing like celebrating Independence Day with baseball," as I said in some form every other year?

All I could think about was the haunting message I had received from my mom at 10:23 a.m.

"We are OK, but shooting at the HP parade. I'm a f***ing mess."

It didn't really sink in, in part because I had become numb to such awful acts of violence in our country and because I didn't know enough details. I didn't realize how close they were to losing their lives. By the time I arrived at the ballpark, I had learned about the unthinkable deaths in my hometown of Highland Park, Illinois, and just wanted to be done with the day. Who could possibly care about baseball? By the time the day finished, I sat alone at the hotel bar, disinterested in going out to celebrate the holiday. Royals infielder Nicky Lopez, a Chicago native himself, walked over to check on me and give me a hug.

GAME

It couldn't end this way. Not for a two-time cancer survivor. Sadly, it did that day for seven innocent souls. The thought of my mom and dad walking in a parade toward the shooter horrified me. The image of them running in the opposite direction was one I couldn't possibly envision even while knowing every step of Central Avenue. I don't ever remember seeing my mother ever run in my life. She was always too busy setting an example of hard work along with my dad for me and my brother. While she never had girls, she laid the foundation for her future granddaughters by saying that women can do anything.

When I told my mother I wanted to write a chapter about her in this book, the defense mechanism of a woman who grew up the middle child with two brothers and the mother of two boys kicked in.

"I have always been the butt of humor among the men in my family. I hope you are not bashing me." We certainly picked on our mother over the years, out of love, of course. Nancy Yelenik was born and raised in New Jersey, the daughter of Irving and Frances Yelenik. My grandfather, who we called Zayda, was born in New York City and went on to become a tool and die maker working in a factory. My grandmother, aka Bubbie, emigrated with her brothers, sister, and parents from Ukraine to Canada in 1929. She went to nursing school in the United States and would be the only one of her siblings to settle in the US. She married my grandfather at nineteen, and rules prohibited her from continuing school while married, so her nursing career ended before it started. She eventually became a teacher and ran a nursery. Irving and Frances had three children and made the nine-hour drive from North Jersey to Montreal to visit family once a month following the end of my grandfather's shift on a Friday. They returned Sunday night in time for him to head back to the factory Monday morning. The importance of hard work, family, and treating people well was set early for my mom and uncles.

As for my mother, "Her passion was music. Practicing the piano, playing glockenspiel in the marching band," my uncle Stephan told me of his older sister.

My uncle Barry, the oldest of the Yelenik siblings, offered me two descriptions from their childhood that dated back some seventy years. "Nancy was always precise. She planned well and liked to take charge."

I can attest to seeing those traits as a child and adult, and Nancy's grandkids would confirm that assessment. We would all agree with Barry's other observation that my mom "always cared heavily about her family."

How my mom managed a successful career while handling two needy sons born nineteen months apart amazes us now, although I'm pretty sure the teenage versions of my younger brother, Marc, and I hardly recognized her superpowers then.

As a parent of two teenage daughters now, Marc accurately reflected on our mother. "Of all the things I've been inspired by and tried to learn from Mom, one of the tops is her incredible ability to somehow keep her important values of family and hard work front and center without having to compromise one for the other. She would find a way to gracefully handle one of our dramatic calls from home as teenagers fighting about something ridiculous or being unable to find something in our home right in front of our eyes without losing her patience."

I'm not sure if our mother dreamed of raising two difficult sons who fought nonstop. I know she didn't envision her ultimate career.

Young Nancy thrived in school and received the kind of grades that should've opened doors in any profession. She went to Montclair State after high school and was told young women should be nurses or teachers. She chose the latter with a focus on music education.

"I picked the best music school within commuting distance, and that's how I proceeded," Mom told me on a Mother's Day podcast we recorded with her as my guest in 2022.

She taught high school music before stepping away to raise Marc and me. I'm sure spending endless time breaking up disputes with her boys provided plenty of motivation to get back to work. She told me a story from my early years that I didn't recall but believe full-heartedly.

"As little guys, I can remember one situation where the two of you were just going at it. And I finally said, 'I've had it. Get up, go to your rooms until you stop fighting.' And you looked at your little brother, and he was a toddler and you were not much more than that. And you took his hand and you said, 'Let's get out of here. We don't like her anyway.'"

Mom eventually decided to return to teaching, but humanities funding, which she would need to continue her music education, had dried up, and the options of being a substitute teacher or maternity leave fill-in did not satisfy her interests. So, she went back to community college to take some math courses and developed an interest in computer programming, a skill we now call coding. Ironic that my brother would eventually work in higher education, including stops at multiple community colleges in

Oregon. Marc and I tagged along as youngsters during the summer while she took classes at Burlington County College.

"I fell in love with the software development, the logic," Mom said. "It was very similar to studying music analysis to me."

She broke into the field but then took time off again as we moved from a Philadelphia suburb in South Jersey to Chicago in 1985 after my dad's job in marketing for a chemical company forced a relocation to the Midwest for a family that only knew the East Coast.

Following the cross-country move, she told herself, "I would wait six months before I even looked for a job so I could get you guys settled. And I would say after about four months in, I started to get really antsy."

Antsy Nancy will always describe a woman who needs to be busy. That holds true today when we visit my parents, who still live in the same house we moved into in 1985. Expect a full itinerary with museums, movies, and more for her grandkids upon arrival. Once again, as Uncle Barry said, "Always precise." If she took off four months back then, I have no recollection. I have vivid memories of thirteen-year-old me showing up for the first day of eighth grade just a few days after we arrived at Highland Park. I knew no one but my brother when I showed up for Mrs. Eytalis's homeroom class, and I wasn't looking for an ally from a sixth grader. I quickly gravitated toward Matt Lickerman and Jeff Weintraub, my two closest friends to this day. Matt had this toy that only an eighth-grade boy could love. A squishy slap hand palm toy that stuck to whatever he threw it at. Like a frog's tongue grabbing bugs, he could throw it and pull anything back. However, Matt took it to another level. He found it amusing to break pieces off and throw them at the ceiling. I was hooked! To this day, Jeff, who now uses his adopted father's name, Landsman, laughs at the memory.

"I remember looking up and seeing tons of sticky parts. And pencils," on the ceiling.

Jeff was my earliest broadcast partner. We made pretend DJ tapes and fake television newscasts in high school. He eventually went on to work for Oprah Winfrey before starting his own production company, Phase6.

I spent many nights at Matt's house watching sports and playing basketball growing up. He's now an emergency room doctor in South Florida and a die-hard Cubs fan. I really despised the Cubs as a teen. That strong dislike was developed at Elm Place Jr. High, where Matt and most of my classmates constantly talked about their Cubbies. I had no choice but to hate the Cubs as an obnoxious thirteen-year-old whose beloved Phillies played in the same division.

I also remember quickly being made fun of for my East Coast accent. A foul in basketball was pronounced "fow-el," not "fal." Orange was "ore-inge," not "ah-ringe," and kids played catch. Asking to "have a catch" could lead to endless ribbing. People still occasionally hear a slight hint of my Philly roots in my accent today, but I quickly adapted to Chicago, minus the Cubs. The Bulls, with a young Michael Jordan, were intoxicating, and the Bears, within months of our arrival, were in the Super Bowl, shuffling their way to a championship.

My earliest memories of living in Chicago are connecting over sports while making new friends, riding bikes all over town, and being latchkey kids, a way of life for most teenagers in the 1980s. So, if my mom took time off, I have limited memories. She and my dad left home to take the train to their downtown offices before we woke up, and they returned around dinnertime.

"Are you going to write about being a latchkey kid in this book?" she wondered. I think that was a rhetorical question.

Mom landed a job with a small company that traded equity options called Chicago Research and Trading. CRT was looking for somebody who could program in a certain language with a financial background. She told them she had no financial background, but she was a heck of a programmer. She began as a software developer on a staff of twenty-five people working in the technology department and left twenty-two years later as a highly successful leader of multiple teams. Her unexpected move into management happened a few years after she began when she was asked to fill in for her boss, who needed heart surgery.

Along the way, NationsBank bought CRT in 1994 and merged with Bank of America in 1998. I remember all the trips she took to Frankfurt, London, Tokyo, Singapore, and Hong Kong. Always on the go and often up in the middle of the night taking phone calls from overseas, she managed multiple teams in different cities, first as principal, senior technology manager of software development and then as principal, senior technology manager of quality assurance.

"It was challenging at times, being the only woman to be able to stand my ground and advocate for my group."

She retired in 2008 and slowed down but never stopped. Bringing her love of music back into her life, she volunteered for the Chicago Symphony Orchestra's Docent Program for six years, visiting schools that didn't have a budget for music with the goal of providing some form of education. More recently, she's been working passionately with her local chapter of the League of Women's Voters. She was walking next to the League's float in the parade on July 4, a block and a half away, heading toward the shooter. Thank goodness she wasn't silenced.

To this day, her younger brother Stephan marvels at my mother's ability to capture the same spirit she had in the 1960s: "She wants to make the world right. She's never lost that desire."

I see so much of my mom in my daughter Ellie and Marc's girls, Maia and Evie, and have heard the girls refer to their grandmother quite simply as a "badass."

POSTGAME

The poor bartender at the hotel that July 4 had no idea what she was getting into when she asked, "How's your day going?" I was numb and in shock, as I drank a couple of glasses of red wine and ate an overpriced cheeseburger. How could this happen in my hometown, and how did my parents survive? When I returned to my room, watching my town on every national news network, I sent Nicky Lopez a text at 10:57 p.m., more than twelve hours removed from the shooting. I rarely text players about my life, choosing to message them only after milestones, personal moments like weddings and the birth of children, or to send condolences after the loss of loved ones. In this case, it was about me. I just wanted to thank him for caring.

"No problem," he replied. "Always here for you and everyone on this team! Baseball is secondary when it comes to things like this. If you ever need anything, let me know." I've believed for a long time that the apple rarely falls far from the tree. I've met Nicky's parents and brothers and, therefore, was not surprised by his reply.

I would like to think the same can be said of me in relation to my parents. In many ways, I'm a clone of my paternal grandfather in terms of appearance and personality. I learned lessons from all four of my late grandparents and am lucky enough to still be inspired by my parents. My mom recently shared with me the lessons she learned from my Zayda.

"As a young girl, I had conversations with my father about hard work, but also about never judging a person before you knew them and giving people a chance to prove themselves or disprove themselves. You accept everyone unless there's something that has disproved them. But that hard work ethic really came from there. And you know, I'm proud of the fact that we handed that down to you and your brother."

8

José Cuas

PREGAME

I've told countless stories on television since beginning my broadcast career in 1994 and somewhere in the thousands during baseball games. Big league debuts never ever get old, as they usually involve the players' families flying in to watch in person, details about phone calls home, tears and disbelief, and recollections about a long journey to the top involving resilience. The elite-level prospects receive massive signing bonuses and a path more easily paved to the majors. No guarantees, but those high-dollar bonuses will afford a young player the benefit of the doubt.

The first overall pick in the 2015 MLB amateur draft, Dansby Swanson, received a signing bonus of $6,500,000 after playing college ball at Vanderbilt University as a twenty-one-year-old shortstop. He made his debut with the Atlanta Braves fourteen months after the draft, ascending quicker than most through the minor leagues. He made more than $20M during seven seasons with Atlanta before signing a seven-year, $177M guaranteed deal with the Chicago Cubs.

The 331st pick in that same draft, another college shortstop, received a $100,000 bonus and played in his first MLB game in 2022 as a pitcher, taking a big-league field for the first time, 2,113 days after Swanson's debut. His story may be the best I ever told on the air.

GAME

The flight left Louisville at about 6:00 a.m. on May 30, 2022. A layover in Chicago preceded a second leg to Omaha. As a bleary-eyed twenty-eight-year-old named José prepared to hit the pillow, the phone rang, informing him of a change of plans. Back to the airport, Omaha to Minneapolis, Minneapolis to Cleveland. A long day of travel but a short trip compared to the journey of a lifetime.

José Cuas dreamed of playing in the big leagues as early as four years old when he could first remember rooting for the New York Yankees. Born in the Dominican Republic (DR), José's family moved to New York City when he was three months old. His mother, Belkys, worked in the cafeteria at a school. His father, José, was a waiter at a restaurant. Raised in a Spanish-speaking household, young José's parents stressed the importance of education as their oldest son left home to attend PS 81 in Queens. He studied English at school and had a chance to practice at home as Mom and Dad learned their second language through their children.

"My job was always school. My parents were big on the only job was to focus on school and then chores around the house," Cuas says.

As a sophomore in high school, he began to excel on the baseball field as a shortstop, receiving recognition from colleges and pro scouts. He began to wonder if he could play professionally, maybe even for his beloved Yankees. The Toronto Blue Jays drafted him in the fortieth round out of Grand Street Campus High School in Brooklyn in 2012. He declined the offer, choosing to attend the University of Maryland on a scholarship. Three years later, the Milwaukee Brewers chose Cuas in the eleventh round of the draft.

He joined thousands of other professionals on fields in smaller stadiums across the United States with shared dreams of playing in the big leagues. He says he "struggled miserably" in his second year but expected to bounce back in 2017.

Cuas' woes continued, so he called his agent and said, "I have no shot as an infielder. I don't want to give up. I have a healthy arm. I want to try pitching."

The Brewers obliged and he went back to the lowest level of the minor leagues and found some early success on the mound before hitting the wall. Milwaukee released Cuas.

"At that point, that's when I wanted to give up," Cuas admits.

His first child, a son, was born amidst José's baseball struggles in April 2018. Ready to move on, his agent called with an opportunity to play independent ball. Cuas signed a ten-day contract in July with the Long Island Ducks in New York and proved himself quickly, earning a longer deal as his confidence "went through the roof." Cuas stuck with the Ducks, pitching in twenty-two games. A far cry from the big leagues, Cuas made about $1,200 a month, cashing a paycheck every other week ranging from $380 to $450. He viewed it as a necessary sacrifice to earn a trip back to a minor league team affiliated with an MLB club.

Cuas hoped to parlay his success into a spot on a Winter Ball team in the Dominican to continue to hone his craft but was cut after a tryout in the DR. Devastated again and struggling to pay the bills, the twenty-four-year-old took a job with FedEx in December 2018, hoping to provide for his family during the busy holiday delivery season. Not exactly his dream, but the pay sure beat independent ball. Making six hundred dollars a week during peak season exceeded any minor league check he ever received. Cuas woke up at 5:00 a.m. daily, arrived at the warehouse by 6:00 a.m., and often made two hundred stops a day delivering over three hundred packages. His dream of delivering strikes began to fade but José's younger brother Alex refused to let the curveballs of life strikeout hopes of stepping on an MLB mound. Alex pitched in college and became his older brother's pitching coach in the most unique circumstances. After arriving home exhausted nightly at 8:00 p.m., José would work out at a park in Queens with Alex in the frigid cold under the one light that worked in the park. Whatever confidence José now lacked was countered by hard work.

The sacrifice paid off as Cuas returned to the Long Island Ducks in 2019 before the Arizona Diamondbacks signed him and sent him to the low levels of the minor leagues.

By 2020, COVID-19 eliminated the minor league season, and Arizona cut Cuas. That release stung because he felt he was finally back on track. He attempted Winter Ball again in 2020 and made the team. José started 2021 with Long Island again but graduated from independent ball when the Kansas City Royals signed him. Back to affiliated minor league ball, Cuas debuted for the Royals' lowest-level team in early July, throwing three perfect innings and striking out six of the nine batters he faced. Eleven days later, the organization springboarded him right past two levels of A-Ball to AA, higher than any step of his career. By the end of the season, he finished with three games at AAA, one step from the Majors.

Fast forward to late May 2022. The former shortstop-turned-FedEx-driver-turned-sidearm-pitcher hopped a commercial flight from Louisville to head home with his Omaha Storm Chasers teammates on an off-day from the chaotic grind of a AAA schedule. Ready to fall asleep upon returning to Omaha, he received the call. He was being summoned to the show. The third and fourth fights of the day would ultimately bring him to Progressive Field in Cleveland with his dream awaiting.

Arriving during the game with his duffle bag, the wiry-built right-hander couldn't figure out how to get into the stadium. He eventually made his way to the visiting clubhouse, suited up, and joined his teammates in the bullpen, nerves aplenty. The team did not need him that night, but he still called home after the game to fill his family in on every detail.

Sitting in his room at the team's fancy hotel, he said to his mom on the phone, "I can't believe I'm here. I think they might make me do the dishes."

Ritz-Carltons were not part of his life or baseball experience until that moment. The next night, another phone rang. It was the bullpen phone. His wife, parents, son, and the newest addition to the family, his baby daughter, made it in time for the Tuesday evening game. So did his brother, who was so instrumental in José's resilient push to the big leagues. After a leadoff single by Cleveland in the fifth inning, Cuas was summoned. I had talked to José before the game and promised my producer, Kevin Cedergren, that José's story would blow him and our audience away.

Kevin gave me the go-ahead to tell the story right out of the commercial break as Cuas finished his warmup tosses, and somehow I crammed a lifetime's worth of a story into a minute and fifteen seconds, starting my report by saying, "It is a debut for José Cuas and this might be the best story we've heard in years."

I may have undersold that statement because I think it's the most amazing story I've ever told in a game. Cuas struck out the first batter and retired all three.

After the game, I hosted our postgame show right by the visiting dugout and watched José's family trickle down to the field to take pictures and congratulate him. He embraced his little brother, the man who never let him give up.

I could hear Alex say, "I told you we would have this moment."

José responded, "Thank you for not letting me quit."

We were in a commercial break and about to return to the air as I tried my best to control the tears. Two months later, I took an Uber from the Royals team hotel in Midtown Manhattan to Yankee Stadium but made a pit stop along the way to Queens. Alex Cuas met me at Joseph Mafera Park, a.k.a. Oval Park. He showed me the one light and the spot on the field where they threw nightly on the grass and sometimes even on the blacktop. From Oval Park to Yankee Stadium, the journey was complete. José had pitched successfully against the feared Bronx Bombers two days earlier, and by the end of that Sunday, he would have pitched again, the local kid who never gave up.

POSTGAME

I told José at the end of the 2022 season that he represented the greatest "don't give up" story.

We were back in Cleveland, where his MLB career began. He thought for a moment and responded, "I'm using my story to reach out to the world. Not even kids, anybody in general. Whatever your dream is, I overcame probably the toughest situation you could possibly overcome being kicked out of the game twice. I went through every tough situation possible, and now I'm in the big leagues."

A truly special delivery from FedEx to the bigs.

9

Jason Benetti

PREGAME

I've been serenaded on the air on multiple occasions. Once on my birthday, Kansas City Royals stars Salvador Perez and Eric Hosmer led a crowded stadium of fans in a sing-along of "Happy Birthday" during a postgame interview. The others occurred numerous times out of the mouth of Chicago White Sox play-by-play announcer Jason Benetti.

As we wrapped up interviewing Benetti at the end of a guest appearance on our *Royals Live* pregame show in the summer of 2018 in Chicago, Jason said, "I have one thing to say to you, Joel." He then proceeded to sing the lyrics of the One Direction song "What Makes You Beautiful."

Sure, it was a "bit" that originally began on a prior pregame show when Jason boldly decided to sing a song dedicated to our director, Steve Kurtenbach, who he had worked with in the past. It became expected that Jason would sing something to end every segment when he guested with us. We laughed so hard every time as the clips made their way to the website Awful Announcing, but these moments meant more to me than just a simple laugh. They said more about Benetti the person who is one of my favorite announcers and people in baseball.

GAME

I asked Jason for a favor in May 2023. A young man named Jack Weafer had asked me to meet Jason before a Royals–White Sox game. I've known Jack since the beginning of my time with the Royals, and at the risk of sounding hyperbolic, I can say Jack knows more about sports than anyone I've ever met. I learned this in our initial encounter in 2008. As I stepped off the elevator at Kauffman Stadium, just weeks into my new job as a completely unknown television personality in Kansas City, I was greeted by an extremely energetic and enthusiastic eleven-year-old in a wheelchair, who belted out what to me eventually became a trademark greeting. "Heyyyyyyy," followed up by questions upon questions along with statements featuring an endless amount of knowledge about games, athletes, umpires, and, during that first meeting, information he had researched about *me*! Now a twenty-six-year-old, the young man with cerebral palsy (CP) wanted to meet his hero, and Benetti obliged.

Here's the thing about Jason. Sports fans all over the country regularly list him as their favorite announcer due to his national work calling college football and basketball. Prior to becoming the TV voice of the Detroit Tigers, White Sox fans treasured the local Chicago kid returning home to call games for his childhood team. He replaced a Southside legend in Ken "Hawk" Harrelson and never missed a beat. Maybe it was the strong voice or love of the game or his deep knowledge of pop culture, which he so smoothly works into his calls. For those of us who know Jason, it may just be the fact that he seems to be everyone's friend and treats every person he encounters warmly and authentically. The fact he has cerebral palsy himself never enters the equation in terms of Jason's credentials as a broadcaster.

I'm always moved by the thoughtfulness in any conversation with Jason, whether about baseball, broadcasting, or life. He summed up to me how the pandemic stole so much of the face-to-face we missed, in and out of sports, with his usual eloquence.

"I tend to think there's got to be something novel about every day. And over the course of 162 games, I struggle with it all being the same," Benetti said. "I really crave the thing that makes this day at the ballpark different. And sometimes that's just in a conversation or a riff or like whatever it is. That's what I love about getting to be in ballparks again."

Walking around stadiums all over the country affords guys like me and Jason so many opportunities to connect with interesting people. Meeting the Jack Weafers of the world makes our day. I can still hear Gloria, the sweet elevator operator in a wheelchair in Cleveland years after her passing, saying, "Have a great day and *enjoy* the game." Ishmael, the jovial hotel shuttle driver in St. Petersburg, always referred to me as "Mr. Joel" year after year. These are the people and moments that energize me as much as any play on the baseball diamond.

I met a boy named Noah Marker at a baseball clinic for kids with disabilities years ago at Kauffman Stadium and we kept in touch via private messages on Twitter season after season. As far as I can tell, the correspondence began in 2017, sometime after getting to know Noah and his family over the years, when the Markers would stop by our postgame set after a Royals game. Despite being confined to a wheelchair his whole life, Noah graduated from a Kansas City suburban high school and attended the University of Missouri, commuting long distances while chasing his dream of being a sports journalist. He would message often to talk about the Royals, tell me about trips to stadiums around the country with his family, and often just to let me know when they planned to come to a game.

I heard from Noah at 3:25 p.m. on July 14, 2023, for the first time in a couple of months. "Hey! We're planning on being at the game tonight," he sent via private Twitter message. "Are you hearing any word about the game being canceled? It seems pretty 50/50 right now."

I responded to Noah and let him know the game would be postponed, which was not public knowledge yet. He thanked me for saving his family a trip to the stadium and, I think, took pride in delivering breaking news to his parents. They showed up for the next game instead and visited us, as always, after the postgame. We chatted with Noah and his little brother Kane and enjoyed a few moments together. Two nights later, seconds before I began an interview for our pregame show, a man handed me a notecard. *Joel Goldberg* appeared on the outside of the folded card. I didn't open it until ten minutes later, after my interview. The inside read:

Joel-

I thought you needed to know this. Noah Marker, Excelsior Springs, passed away today. I know you and Noah had a close relationship.

—friend of the family-Doug

Needless to say, I was stunned and broke the news to Monty moments before our show started. Doug had left his number on the card for me to call if I wanted to verify. After following up, I asked Doug to please share my cell phone with the Markers if they needed me to help in any way.

Walking through Manhattan a week later during a Royals trip to face the Yankees, I received a text from Noah's father, Marty, that would lead to one of the biggest honors of my life.

"If you're available next Saturday, we would be honored if you would be a pallbearer for our sweet Noah. If you can't, we totally understand. Your relationship with Noah was special."

The Royals were scheduled to play a night game at home, so with no conflicts, I replied yes within seconds and walked into the Excelsior Springs High School auditorium eight days later.

Noah's mom, Christy, asked me to say goodbye to Noah before the service.

"He wanted to be you," she said as I looked down at her son.

That's when the tears began. I kept repeating what she said in my head as I walked away from the casket. "He wanted to be you." Noah's older brother, Andy, delivered an emotional and beautiful eulogy, sharing so many special memories, and he even mentioned stories involving Noah and me. Tears trickled down my face as the woman to my left and the man to my right, both pallbearers and strangers to me, handed me tissues simultaneously. I knew at that moment that my dreams of being a broadcaster turned out so much better than I could've ever imagined. It just took heartache to see it. I'm not sure I understood how special my relationship with Noah was until he was gone. As I sat through the celebration, I reflected on the power of my job and the impact it can often make on others in profound ways. This is what Benetti had so eloquently described on my podcast.

Everything we do is about people and relationships. Fostering those connections with fans, players, coaches, and executives every day is small ball at its greatest. The fact Jason did that in the ballpark he regularly attended as a kid is icing on the cake, or sundae, if you will. When he walked into Guaranteed Rate Field during his time with the White Sox, he often found himself thinking, *Ballpark still smells like I remember, right? I know where I used to get the helmet sundae. That is a sensory thing that will never go away. And I just know my way around the park, and I know what Sox fans are like because I was around them for a long time.*

That kid eating the helmet sundae dreamed of calling Sox action. In third grade, he wrote about wanting to be the next voice of the White

Sox, just like Hawk Harrelson. Fast forward about twenty-five years, and the dream came true.

"The most amazing part of that to me is that he was the guy that was still doing it when I came of an age where I could do it," Benetti reflected. "I think about this quite often, about things that I say on TV or when walking by people on a concourse. As a child, or even a young adult, the smallest, dumbest, most infinitesimally tiny experiences can make you do a career. I grew up watching Hawk. And so, I was like, all right, I'm going to be a sports announcer."

As a senior in high school, Jason toured the Sox broadcast booths, sitting next to radio announcers Ed Farmer and John Rooney.

"They were very kind to me, and you have these early experiences. And it either pushes you toward or away from a career, and I think about that a lot . . .. I'm gonna say something tonight that might make somebody love baseball forever or hate it. I think that is our charge. And it's not a burden. But that's the distinctly important thing we can do on a nightly basis without even realizing it."

Dreams indeed can become reality and when they involve a deeper purpose, they can be incredibly fulfilling. The fact he does it all with cerebral palsy is part of the story, just not the full story. It's why I didn't bring up CP when Jason appeared on *Rounding the Bases* in 2022 until more than a half hour passed. I mentioned this to him, about being judged by his talents.

"It's so layered," Benetti responded. "I tend to think inspiration is what people decide it is . . .. So if I'm inspirational for somebody, I hope it's in hiring somebody who they made a first judgment about and they were wrong about, or something like that."

Or, digging into his many pop culture references, Benetti put it this way: "Jerry Seinfeld has talked about comedy as basically totally egalitarian. Like, if you're funny, they're gonna laugh. And if they laugh, they're gonna hire you again. And if they continue to laugh, they'll hire you again. And that's the end of it. There's nothing else in there. It's just, are you good? Or aren't you? And my whole deal the whole time I've been doing this has been, make the work good enough that they just can't say no, for whatever superficial reason."

As a young boy, he carried a different perspective, as we all did without the benefit of time and maturity.

"I never wanted to identify as a person with a disability . . . I probably thought of it as, like, I don't want to be one of the misfits, right, like I wanted to fit in very badly."

What Jason once avoided is part of who he is today, even if it doesn't define him.

"I've realized over the set of circumstances that is my life that the thing you actually want to be is different than other people. You want to be unique; you want to add value in some way that other people don't. And so I get to have that built-in."

Maybe that's the burden, yet he always manages a healthy, if not amusing, perspective, thanks to his entertaining love of pop culture. Sitting in the exit row on a plane once, the flight attendant asked him three times if he could handle the responsibilities without sharing a similar concern with an elderly couple.

"You got like Rue McClanahan and her husband across. I know she's passed, but pick any of the Golden Girls with her husband. And they're like eighty-five, and it's like, 'Oh, they've got this. They're fine.' And me? I know. Yeah, no chance. I'm not saving anybody in 15D."

So, what's Jason's role or responsibility in the public eye as a man living with cerebral palsy? His answer, to no surprise, is layered and involves another TV show.

"RJ Mitte of *Breaking Bad*, Walt Jr., has CP. And he has a different version of it than I do and his speech is more affected than mine. And he walks differently than I do. But that's fantastic. Because I can be a sports announcer with CP, but I'm not on camera very much . . . I think often actually about kids, like if I were young again, and I were to have seen RJ Mitte on *Breaking Bad*, would I have thought, *oh, maybe I should be an actor?*"

Benetti embraces the potential impact.

"When I was a kid, there was nobody with CP on television. And so to be a person with CP on television, I think is important. Because especially in an era where just about everybody has a role model on TV, of the color, of the gender, of the sexual orientation. I think that's really becoming very important for people to say, especially for parents to say, hey, there's reason not to give up; there's reason to continue on and to do the tough stuff. I think that can be important."

With that said, he's hesitant to be the spokesperson.

"I also am very wary of speaking for, quote-unquote, the disability community on the whole. Because I know there are a lot of people who have more substantial physical problems in a major way than by a multiplier of one hundred than I do. I've met some kids with CP who are nonverbal, who use wheelchairs, and use eye gaze technology to speak."

When we approached the elevator to go down one floor to visit Jack Weafer, Jason asked me if I wanted to take the stairs, and I remembered what he had told me on the podcast about one of his colleagues on White Sox radio.

"Len Kasper and I joke a lot because he didn't realize what it's like to go around with me . . . Len and I'll go grab a bite to eat or something. And he marvels at the hit rate of the amount of times I get asked if I need an elevator when there's a staircase involved. Like people just want to know if I want an elevator. And they're being considerate, but it gets repetitive for me."

We walked down the stairs and met Jack and his father, Tom, in the lobby at Kauffman Stadium.

"Heyyyyy," Jack belted out and proceeded to quiz Jason on game after game, story after story.

I marveled at Jason's genuine interest as he repeatedly asked Jack, "What else do you want to know?"

Mindful of Jason's time, I kept my eye on the clock as the recording time for his TV open with Steve Stone rapidly approached. He never flinched and patiently engaged and listened for a half hour as he made Jack's day. The power of one person's dream can affect so many others, and I was privileged to witness it firsthand.

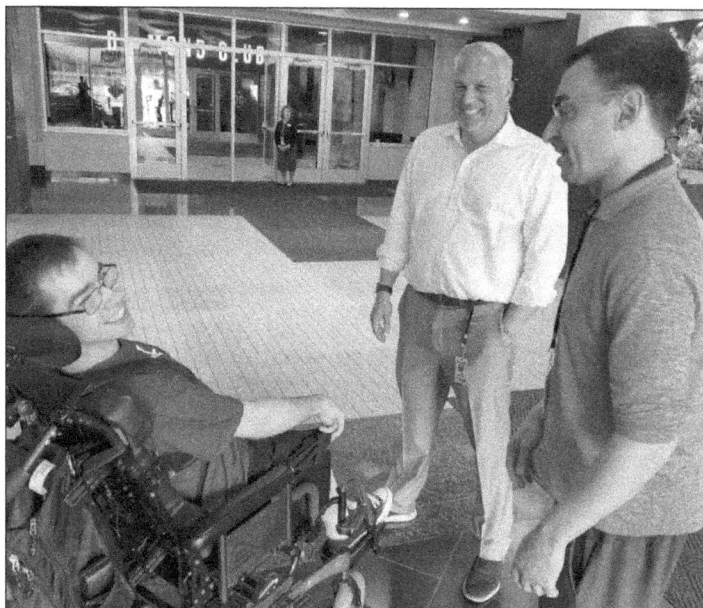

A year later, Jason returned to Kauffman Stadium in his new role as the Detroit Tigers play-by-play man and I brought him down to see Jack again in the lobby. A new team, a new job, but the same incredible dynamic watching these two talk life and sports.

POSTGAME

The year 2021 saw the return to a full season of baseball, but radio and television crews across MLB still did not travel. A recorded interview with Jason Benetti via Zoom was the best we could do to see our good friend and share his insight and wit with a Royals TV audience.

I mentioned missing him, and he said, "I was sitting at home during the two off days, and I was thinking, *my gosh, it has been so long since I've seen you guys.* I mean, we're not traveling to start the year, and I was just like, you know what? We do Sox math on our telecast. Let me just total it up, and I couldn't believe that."

He set up another bit and then transitioned into his singing voice, channeling his inner Broadway as he belted out his version of the song "Seasons of Love" from the musical *Rent.*

I informed Jason that maybe Monty would sing along if it was The Eagles. He did not know this inquiry was coming. Never one to miss a moment, he pivoted and serenaded us with, "Don't you draw the queen of diamonds, boy," from the hit "Desperado." From Don Henley to Broadway, baseball to basketball, pop culture aficionado to role model, Jason Benetti is living a dream and helping bring joy to others every step of the way. I'm trying to do the same, minus the singing.

10

Laura "Fancy" Sanko

PREGAME

The music was thumping—just what you would expect on a night out at one of Kansas City's premiere entertainment districts. The sounds of clinking glasses and socializing patrons slowly drowned out the higher notes, leaving only the low, familiar tone of bass reverberating throughout the space. It was one the accomplished musician recognized well, albeit a different flavor of the instrument she knew so well.

Can you ever escape the familiarity of something you pour so many hours into, even on a fun night out with friends? Laura Sanko had mastered piano as a kid, demonstrating the focus and dedication that are all but required to command the ivory keys . . . or anything else she decided to set her mind to.

Laura always knew what she was made of, but we can be glad that at the time not everyone did. Otherwise, the acquaintance she ran into that evening may have used a different tone when the petite, sports car–driving blonde shared her news. She had signed up for her first mixed martial arts fight.

"Honey, don't bother yourself trying to do this sport," he scoffed. "You're too fancy."

Those words and a dismissive attitude were all it took for the challenge to be issued.

"I am fancy," she conceded before adding, "*and* I can fight." A fiery conviction flashed as she spoke the words. What's more is that she didn't just promise to fight; she *did* fight. And she won.

GAME

When Laura "Fancy" Sanko's incredible journey to become the first female color commentator in the Ultimate Fighting Championship (UFC) history began, it looked different than it does today. To call it lucky would understate all of the hard work that went into earning her groundbreaking role, and it certainly wasn't the dream she had initially set out to achieve.

She grew up in a devout Christian household that placed a high priority on traditional family values. Academically, she had always been incredibly gifted but had been raised to believe that a woman's highest purpose in life was to be married and become a mother. Daring to dream of anything bigger simply was not part of the discussion. Imagining a world where she was the one to break down barriers in the niche sport of ultimate fighting was out of the question.

For years, Laura kept close to the path expected of her. She behaved, attended regular church services, and studied hard at her small, private school. After years of earning top marks, she earned the highest distinction any graduating student could hope for: being named the class valedictorian. Naturally, she also performed exceptionally well on her ACT, scoring an impressive thirty-four. She recognized it was impressive in real-time, but it took a couple of decades' worth of hindsight to understand just how much so.

Her scores alone would have been enough to earn her a scholarship to any of the colleges she was interested in. Even with a strong case of self-proclaimed performance anxiety, her exceptional piano skills still managed to eclipse her intellect. Ultimately, the scholarship she accepted was for music. Achieving that level of excellence in any pursuit demands focus, timing, movement control, and a work ethic. Pianists must also demonstrate exceptional attention to detail and mental fortitude. On the surface, classical instruments and combat sports couldn't be more different. When broken down to the basics, though, they're more similar than you might expect. And it laid a strong foundation as she grew into herself.

As is often the case, young Laura showed interest in a range of activities and dabbled in many of them. Unlike most, the spirit of competition is woven so deeply into the cloth of who she is as a person that few undertakings were ever purely recreational.

"I grew up doing karate," she told me. "I was not overly competitive at it," she said of the sport she continued to pursue because of the mental clarity it gave her.

It's also an ironically humble assessment of her involvement, considering she went on to earn her black belt. Most of all, it's a perfect illustration of her innate competitiveness. No matter what lane you put her in, she always looks for a way to pull ahead of the pack, even if her biggest competition is herself. In the future, it would prove to be a valuable skill.

Given the focus, drive, and athleticism that were always unassuming pillars of Laura's story, it shouldn't come as a surprise that she went on to become a champion at anything. Truth be told, she was one all along, even if—judging by appearances—mixed martial arts wasn't the obvious place for her to land. What stands out to me the most about her story is how she always managed to fight her way to the top, even in pursuits she had no experience in. Or when pitted against others who—on paper—had every qualification she lacked, especially when she thought she had failed, she would realize she had prevailed again.

After college, life threw Laura a few more punches than usual. She remembers thinking, *I need something to take my mind off of the hot mess dumpster fire that is my life right now.*

She also remembered how great karate training always used to make her feel and sought to reclaim the same high when she joined a mixed martial arts (MMA) gym. The environment was intense. Many of her peers competed regularly, and even though—at the time—Laura didn't, the fervid training sessions had the effect that she had hoped for. It didn't take long before she was encouraged to compete in a real fight so that one day she could tell her grandkids that she did it.

In the same kind of way that last words have a tendency to become famous, she signed up for "just one" match. Not everyone took her seriously. They thought she was too new, too pretty, and too different from the other fighters to ever succeed at such a macho sport. As true competitors so often do, they turn naysaying voices into fuel for the fire. And as good Christian girls like Fancy do, they keep hand gestures to themselves and let their performance do the talking, which you could argue is even more impactful. One time in the ring was all it took.

"There is no better drug than subduing another human being with essentially your bare hands," she said. "As soon as that happened, I was like, I'm done. I'm in. Let's do this more."

Her professional fighting career turned out to be short-lived. She won four of five amateur bouts before winning her first and only pro fight. Impending motherhood and lack of prospects as an atomweight contender influenced her decision to retire from the ring. Instead, despite a complete absence of formal experience, she set her sights on becoming a broadcaster to remain close to the sport she loved and knew so well.

Mixed martial arts is a unique discipline. Its passionate fanbase is niche, yet the sport itself is simultaneously mainstream. The brand was built almost entirely on a distinctly alpha male mentality that few—if any—others were. But it is also one of the rare sports where men and women train and compete alongside each other, despite its macho persona. In fact, women are some of the biggest stars in UFC, oftentimes fighting on higher cards than their male counterparts.

Fancy had the experience and the technical expertise. And even though the timing was right to introduce a female commentator into the MMA broadcasting mix, convincing people to give her a shot proved to be one of her toughest adversaries.

"I didn't go to school for journalism or broadcasting, and I had no experience doing it before I started working for MMA," she said of breaking into television. "I just did my best. And what I always leaned into was my knowledge of the sport."

She pursued her trailblazing role with eyes wide open, recognizing that the bar for women is always set higher, especially when you are making history. Instead of focusing on the stakes at hand, she invested her energy into doing the job right with the best intentions. It worked, and before long, she achieved the biggest victory of her career: respect for a job exceptionally well done.

POSTGAME

Laura Sanko's dreams look different today than when she was younger. Sure, the core values she was raised to believe in are still important to her. But she's come to acknowledge that she was meant to be more than a wife and a mom. Instead, she's accepted the unique privilege of charting a new course. And in doing so, she proved that she isn't just a fighter who became a champion; she's a champion because she is a fighter in everything she does—especially for women in the world of sports.

11

Brian Roberts

PREGAME

The pursuit of the dream comes with twists and turns. For most of us, it also brings a handful of defining moments. Sometimes, you can realize them happening in real time, but often, it's not until you look back that you see certain decisions for what they were and recognize the magnitude of their impact.

When Brian Roberts decided to coach a youth soccer team, he submitted his application along with a request to lead a team of high school boys. In return, the former collegiate soccer star was assigned to a team of nine-year-old girls. It may not have been what he had hoped for, but in hindsight, the unseen opportunity drew on his past to define his future and every dream that would come after.

GAME

The first time I met Brian was over lunch. Along with our shared love of sports and business, we had several mutual contacts who suggested we get to know each other. It should have come as no surprise that we hit it off, but I was immediately struck by the warmth of his personality. As I walked away from our meeting, I was floored by the events that led to it happening.

As a kid growing up in the inner city of Los Angeles, sports had always played a central role in Brian's life. They came second only to education, which was always the focus. After the Rodney King riots of 1992, the tone of the community began to change. An increase in violence prompted Brian's parents to relocate the family from their South-Central neighborhood to the Inland Empire.

"My parents made what I now understand were huge sacrifices to move us out," Brian said of his parents' decision. "It changed the types of schools we went to and changed the types of sports that we ended up playing." He continued, "That move was the foundation of everything that's happened since."

Before he called the suburbs home, basketball and football had been mainstays in Brian's life, along with baseball on a lesser scale. Soccer, on the other hand, had never been a part of the family's sports repertoire. Sure, he had heard of it, but he never played until the day he saw some classmates in a match.

"I went to recess, and they were playing soccer," he told me.

He joined and immediately realized his affinity for a game he knew nothing about that morning. It took a chance encounter, but in an instant, Brian wasn't just a kid on the playground. He was a kid with a dream . . . and he was intent on pursuing it.

With as much zeal as any kid who had happened upon something incredible, Brian bounded home, eager to tell his dad everything. Soccer had suddenly become a big deal in his life, and he was eager to learn as much as he could about it. I can only assume he was crushed when he heard his dad's initial reaction.

"We're not going to play soccer," he remembers being told. Even then, he knew this was worth fighting for and didn't relent until his parents had been persuaded. Looking back, it also foreshadowed his rare tenacity that would help shape his future successes.

By today's standards, Brian got a late start in his sport of choice, but his raw talent helped him advance quickly. He soon earned himself a spot on an elite club team that was diverse even for the melting pot that is Southern California. The team was an anomaly in the predominantly white world of club soccer, which created a unique opportunity to hone his skills, both on and off the field. Sports teaches you the game, but it also teaches lessons organically simply by being part of the process. Oftentimes, we hear of the more obvious benefits, such as the value of trust, being a team player, or dealing with defeat. In Brian's case, he was confronted with navigating racism alongside many who had never been faced with that kind of adversity in their lives.

"The first time I was called the N-word was on the soccer field," he told me of his experience as a teenager. "It was even very interesting to see how not only the other African American players dealt with that, but also the white kids who had never had to deal with racism."

In the moment, it was a powerful learning opportunity as the individual players found alignment between themselves and composure against their competitors. Now, it's a seamless part of his story that continued to develop more cohesively than he ever could have imagined.

After high school, Brian's rising soccer stardom, coupled with his academic excellence, enabled him to chart a new path for himself across the country. More specifically, at Yale University in New Haven, Connecticut, he enrolled with the dream of becoming a neurologist. He suddenly found himself in a community where he was more of a minority than he had ever been in his life. By leaning on the experiences he had as a younger player, he also managed to shine brighter than ever.

As a teenager, he had been one of five African Americans on his team. Now, he was one of three. Yet again, he earned a starting position in every game during his four years on the roster. Ivy League demographics outnumbered him multiple times to one, but he excelled academically, earning admission to medical school. In another pivotal life moment, he was drafted to play defender for the Kansas City Wizards Major League Soccer team. With so many incredible opportunities in quick succession, you can't help but wonder how many of them would have been possible had his entire childhood been spent in Los Angeles's urban core.

No matter the neighborhood, one constant had always been academics. His medical pursuits contrasted starkly against Brian's new dream of becoming a professional athlete.

"I remember calling my parents, telling them that I was going to defer my med school to go play soccer," he told me, continuing, "You can imagine what they said."

He was a young adult at the time but had already demonstrated his commitment to pursuing the decisions he knew were right for him, as well as a certain diplomacy in mitigating differences of opinion. Fast forward four years and he made the decision to allow his med school admission to lapse entirely.

When I asked him what that was like, he admitted, "That was one of the greatest decisions that I made throughout the journey."

For anyone unfamiliar with the economics of professional soccer, the lifestyle it affords its players is a far cry from the glitz and glamor of football or baseball. In fact, many players refer to it as a full-time job with part-time pay that, for all but an exclusive few, almost always necessitates a second income source—especially when faced with mounting student loan debt from an Ivy League university. So, it may sound strange that he would reflect on his decision to trade a lucrative career in medicine to continue chasing a dream. But it didn't take long for Brian to face this reality in a decision that brought every dream, success, and adversity he had ever faced into a cumulative, defining opportunity.

As it turns out, his soccer career wasn't where he needed to look. It was in a room full of parents, who had gathered—at his request—to discuss their nine-year-old daughters, whom he coached.

"If you've been a part of youth sports, you know all parent meetings are interesting," he said.

At the time, he was a relative newcomer to Kansas City and not yet familiar with who was who in the business community. Because of it, he had no way of knowing that one of the most prominent and influential businessmen in town, Ron Lockton, was mere feet from him, watching carefully as he deftly navigated a room running high with emotions. Still, Brian's handling of the situation managed to wow Ron. Brian was invited to apply those skills at Ron's namesake, Lockton Insurance, the powerhouse global insurance brokerage.

The decision to walk away from professional soccer to pursue a career in insurance operations wasn't made overnight. However, when the time came to discuss it in more detail, it didn't take long for Brian to realize Lockton was where he would go on to thrive and find his greatest successes.

"I can't see myself pivoting anywhere else," he shared, in evident disbelief that he's already been there for fifteen years. "It's a quietly dynamic industry that I've found myself in and allows me to do all the things that I love to do."

In his tenure, he has grown from an industry outsider to an inextricable leader whose name is almost as synonymous with the success of Lockton Companies as those of its founders. Brian was recently named the COO of the Lockton Midwest Series, overseeing operations in St. Louis, Detroit, Minneapolis, and more from his new office in Chicago. Using the same warm personality that first greeted me, he's earned a reputation that precedes him in all echelons of the business. And no matter the success, it all comes back to the lessons he learned playing soccer.

"I can't even describe how much I've learned from the sport. Whether that be being on a team, being the captain of a team," he told me, "so much of leadership is about influence and speaking to your audience. And it provides every day, provides me, another great lesson."

POSTGAME

The thing about dreams is that we all have them. Some are old and not yet fulfilled, the kind we can never quite let go because they're so full of hope. They keep us going. Others are new, created from the process of growth and discovery that is inevitable with time. What is nearly guaranteed for any kind of dream is that some part of it will play out differently than we imagined. And for some, like Brian Roberts, the reality is even better.

12

Kevin Youkilis

PREGAME

Baseball has always brought people together during good times and, more importantly, during the worst of times. On multiple occasions, I witnessed the impact of the sport on a community at Fenway Park in Boston as a visiting reporter. First in 2004, as the Red Sox opened the World Series at home against the St. Louis Cardinals on the way to ending an eighty-six-year championship drought. I can still feel the energy decades after the Series. Four years later, I stood in the camera well down the third-base line at Fenway and took my earpiece out in the ninth inning to just soak in the crowd's noise. Jon Lester had completed a no-hitter against Kansas City, making for a memorable night even if the postgame show lacked good highlights for a Royals broadcaster. Red Sox slugger David "Big Papi" Ortiz was there for both of those special moments, as he was during the most difficult of circumstances in 2013.

I watched in person as the larger-than-life designated hitter with jewelry that matched his massive smile and giant frame addressed an emotional sold-out crowd at Fenway on April 20, 2013. On this day, Red Sox fans saw their team play its first home game following the Boston Marathon bombing. The tragedy occurred five days earlier, and the Kansas City

Royals were the first opponent to play at Fenway after a rattled city spent the week processing the fear, confusion, and nightmare of the tragedy at a massive public event. The Royals traveled from Atlanta after a day game on Wednesday of that week and landed in Boston during the evening. An off-day Thursday and a postponement of the scheduled Royals–Red Sox game Friday due to the manhunt meant we were sequestered in our hotel for more than two days. We caught glimpses of Anderson Cooper, Wolf Blitzer, and all of the national news personalities, who descended upon Boston and stayed at our hotel to cover the ongoing story.

My two lasting memories occurred Friday evening and Saturday. My wife Susan and I ventured out with a group to Daisy Buchanan's, a legendary local bar, after hearing about the game postponement. I don't know how we managed to do this during a lockdown, but I remember the usual five-minute walk from the hotel taking more than twenty minutes because we had to circumvent such a massive crime scene. We weren't the only ones. A packed venue full of somber, if not sober, patrons tried to lift each other's spirits. I will never forget the reaction to the place, which felt something like being on the set of *Cheers* when the televisions at the bar showed live coverage of the bombing suspect being caught. The place erupted with a sense of pride that flowed as strongly as the beer, although none compared to the next day at Fenway.

A giant US flag was draped over the famous Green Monster wall in left field. First responders were honored, and both teams stood along the foul lines, giving Fenway the feeling of a World Series game in April. The mood felt more like a celebration of life as the first responders walked off the field following their heroic recognition. Big Papi took the microphone.

"All right, Boston," Papi said, prompting nearly ten seconds of applause from those three words. "This jersey that we wear today, it doesn't say Red Sox. It says Boston."

There was more applause, and then Papi went on to thank the governor, mayor, and police officers before sending the proud audience into a frenzy.

"This is our f***ing city, and nobody's going to dictate our freedom. Stay strong; thank you."

The Dominican-born Boston superstar walked off with a hand raised in the air. One of the best sports towns in America boasts so many sports heroes: Ted Williams, Larry Bird, Bobby Orr, Tom Brady, Big Papi, and more, including Kevin Youkilis.

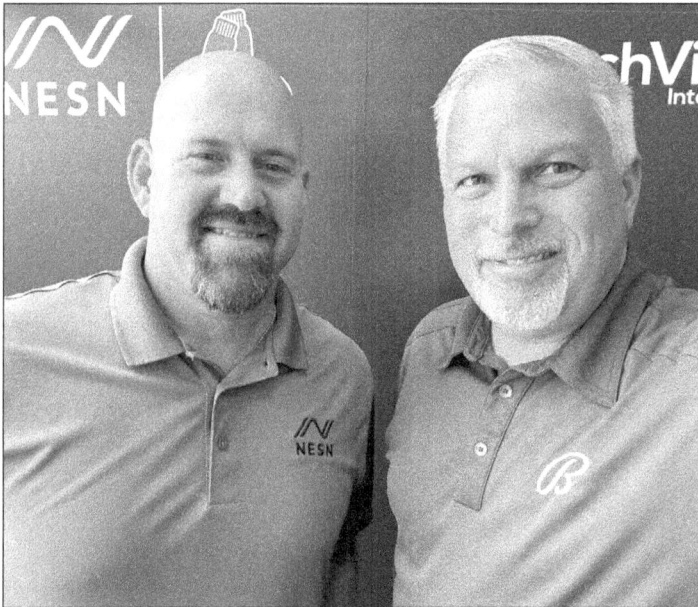

GAME

Youkilis broke into the big leagues in 2004, playing sparingly in that World Series before working his way into a significant role with the Sox 2007 World Championship team. By 2013, when Ortiz made his speech, Youkilis had left New England, finishing his final year as a ballplayer with the Yankees. Still beloved to this day in Boston as a television analyst and

Sox legend, a simple mention of the name Youkilis is likely to prompt a fan to chant, "Yoooooouk."

I first laid eyes on Youkilis briefly in the 2004 World Series while I worked for the St. Louis Fox television affiliate. Like most baseball fans, I knew the name due to the successful 2003 book *Moneyball: The Art of Winning an Unfair Game.* Author Michael Lewis wrote about the Oakland A's competing with higher budget franchises by identifying undervalued players who possessed skills that were overlooked by other teams. General Manager Billy Beane relied on sabermetrics over traditional scouting and emphasized on-base and slugging percentages over traditional metrics like batting average and RBI (runs batted in) in trying to find players. Beane, as written about in the book, wanted to trade for a young Red Sox prospect named Kevin Youkilis because of his penchant in the minor leagues to get on base. Beane gave the former eighth-round pick of the Red Sox the nickname "The Greek God of Walks." It stuck with fans even though he was not Greek and never played for Oakland.

By the time Youkilis carved a name out for himself beyond *Moneyball,* he could be relied upon for bringing a blue-collar style of play to work along with one of the most unique batting stances in MLB history. His crouch in the batter's box looked like one of his idols growing up, Pete Rose. The 6'1" third baseman would loosely hold the bat straight over his head, slightly pointing it toward the pitcher. If the swing yielded contact, fans could expect all-out effort running to first or a brisk circling of the bases after hitting a home run. All of it is from the "Charlie Hustle" way of playing the game that most kids grew up with in Southwestern Ohio in the 1980s.

"Pete had an influence on all the ballplayers in Cincinnati around that time because your dads only knew of him," Youkilis told me. "So you had to play the game that way. If you didn't, you were a dog so it was ingrained in our childhood. Hustle, play hard, and be gritty."

That grit fit perfectly with so many hard-nosed Red Sox players who captured the hearts of a blue-collar fanbase in Boston. Teamed up with the undersized and equally hard-nosed Dustin Pedroia, Youk and "Pedey" encapsulated the gritty mentality of Beantown. Youkilis remembered the second baseman's mindset after an unsuccessful at bat.

"Dustin Pedroia and I used to always laugh because he'd come back. He'd strike out or something and be like, 'The guy stinks,' right before I would go up to bat, and I'm laughing, but that was the attitude that Dustin had. That's the attitude I had, and we weren't the most talented guys physically and all that, but we had the mental process of really going about it in that direction."

It's an attitude that has served him well after baseball, where he now serves suds and has transformed from the Greek God of Walks to the Greek God of Hops.

Youkilis began exploring his second career when the craft beer industry just started to explode. Curious about the industry, Youk went from a world of baseball stats like OPS (on-base percentage plus slugging percentage) to postgame IPAs (India pale ales), taking advantage of the MLB travel life to explore places like Kansas City.

"One of my favorite parts about the visiting clubhouse was after the game; I could get myself a Boulevard brew, and I just really just fell in love with it. I fell in love with talking to brewery owners, talking to brewers, understanding there's like this huge camaraderie between craft brewers. It's the small dogs versus the big dogs."

He went from being a big deal with the Red Sox to the little guy, opening Loma Brewing Company in the San Jose, California area. That gritty, blue-collar attitude birthed in Cincinnati and mastered in Boston served him well trying to create a name amidst a world of juggernauts like Anheuser-Busch, Coors, and Miller as he fought for shelf space the way he did playing time early in his baseball career. His world champion manager Terry Francona's influence can now be seen in Youkilis's leadership style.

"Baseball and beer are always about people, like any other profession. The best managers in any business really sit down and get to know their employees, and also don't hire for that position. They hire for the person and their abilities and their personality that can fit in best with the team," Youkilis said.

Youk saw first-hand the power of blending different personalities into a winning mix with the Red Sox. The twenty-five-year-old made his MLB debut on May 15, 2004, for the Boston Red Sox in Toronto, batting eighth and playing third base. His first hit came in his second at-bat and went over the wall in left field for the first of 150 career big league home runs. Little did he know he would be a World Champion less than half a year later. A team that considered itself a group of lovable idiots gelled perfectly on the field to reverse the infamous "Curse of the Bambino," giving New England its first World Series win since 1918 when Babe Ruth pitched for the Sox and was sold to the rival New York Yankees in 1920. Youkilis vividly remembers his rookie team, who became heroes in Boston.

"There was a group of guys, and they wanted to have fun, and they wanted to enjoy the game. And the different personalities off the field or in the clubhouse, guys would hang out in different groups, but when those lights went on, that group of guys knew how to compete together."

He learned an early lesson about chemistry, witnessing the imperfections of any collection of human beings and the unique ability of certain groups to overcome adversity, even while not being best friends.

"That's no different than a business. Because when you put fifty people together in a business, not everyone's going to agree or get along . . . but if you have the same goals, when it comes to game time, that is the key to success."

The days of slamming a batting helmet in frustration or screaming in the heat of battle now manifest in different ways than the fiery attitude seen in a baseball dugout.

"I've had many different incidents where I've had to hold back and really calm down, and I had to really think through my thoughts . . .. And you always have to be ready because that one moment can really define who you are or your business . . . you have to learn how to suck up your ego, take your pride out of it, and go apologize for your mistake right away."

He sees the business books like the stats of a baseball player. They cannot be manipulated or changed overnight. A dry spell may feel like a slump on the diamond. Patience, curiosity, and attention to detail matter. A hitter batting .180 in June cannot raise his average to .300 overnight. So what can he do to chip away and see gains the rest of the season for himself or his team? It's no different than a tough stretch at the brewery.

"I can't start taking my P&L statement, and all of a sudden, I'm gonna show positives within one day. So you have to think long term, and you have to do little things. Everything's about little, little wins. Sometimes time is our worst enemy in our head because we think we're fighting this deadline instead of just taking it slow and making slow strides," Youkilis told me.

He views hot streaks the same way. It's not a license to go all in but an opportunity to make small gains instead of just wanting to hit more home runs.

"I call it the ocean waves versus lake waves. Do you want lake waves or ocean waves as a season? I want the small waves as much as possible. I want the pond effect. And it's no different in business, too. When you start getting that roller coaster ride, the days get longer; the job gets harder. And you just have to stick within what you're doing and figure out little things each day that can put you in a better spot for tomorrow."

When he's not busy with the brewing business, he's serving up baseball to Red Sox fans as a television analyst, working games with veteran announcer Dave O'Brien. Baseball, beer, and broadcasting all see the same Youk.

"That's him. Just everything at 125 percent. He doesn't know anything other than fifth gear," O'Brien told me outside the Sox TV booth. "And that's the business side of it. That's the broadcast side of it. You know what he was like as a player. That's Kevin Youkilis. That's the essence of who the guy is."

Youkilis believes professional athletes play the game for different reasons, whether money, fame, or competition. Finding a why or purpose, as is so often discussed in the business world, varies with ballplayers, but the goal is always to win a championship. So how does the athlete-turned-entrepreneur motivate his employees, knowing they most likely did not dream of working at his brewery the way he dreamt of playing in the big leagues? His message to them before opening on day one addressed that challenge.

"This might not be your dream job. And I totally get that. Be honest with us. Come to me and say, 'Hey, I got this other job,' and I'm gonna give you a high five and a hug, and I'm super happy that you're moving on to other things. But while you're here, just give us your best. Give us all your effort, give as much as you can to the business. And good things will happen through that."

Bottom line: he loves producing good craft beer. Kind of like winning a big playoff game or a championship, doing so involves strong teams. Youk's true purpose comes from helping his employees grow. He knows he may need to step in and be forceful in certain situations but prefers an approach with less micromanaging and more empathy and encouragement.

"The purpose of what I love every day when I come in here is watching really good people interact in the hospitality business and putting a smile on people's faces . . . You just see people coming together and enjoying that pint of beer. And that, to me, is a lot of fun to watch."

POSTGAME

I ask every podcast guest about their greatest home run professionally. The caveat for a ballplayer is that it can be on or off the field. Youkilis fondly remembered that homer in his MLB debut off Blue Jays veteran Pat Hentgen. The other favorite came off superstar lefty CC Sabathia in the first inning to spark the Red Sox's second world championship in 2007

After losing three straight to Cleveland and trailing the playoff series three games to one, Youk took Sabathia deep in the first inning of game five of the American League Championship Series, and the Red Sox won 7-1. It was the first of seven straight victories en route to a World Series title.

His "home runs" in business may garner less publicity, but they resonate as deeply. Simply put, it's the successful hires that lead to sustainable success. "It's the people within that are the home runs," serving up the suds one customer at a time.

13

Tech N9ne

PREGAME

My *Rounding the Bases* podcast on November 30, 2021, began with the usual written intro about the guest and then some hip-hop music with the lyrics:

> "Like I didn't have this new watch
> And it never would tic and never do toc.
> Like I'm rapping myself to learning brew hops.
> Rapping like I ain't never did a record with 2Pac.
>
> Like I ain't rich, like I ain't sold.
> Not a ne'er record Platinum no ne'er Gold.
> Like I ain't tripped, like I ain't froze.
> Like I ain't made a quarter mill' for a show."

As I played the song "Like I Ain't," I was the only one who could see my guest in the virtual green room of my online podcast recording platform, dancing in his seat to his music like he was hearing a hit song for the first time. I had never met the man but I immediately formed an initial impression of Tech N9ne: hard-working, passionate, and high energy. As the platinum recording artist rode on his tour bus from Memphis to

New Orleans, he refused to postpone this podcast appearance, even while losing his voice as a seventy-seven-city schedule of concerts over three months neared completion.

I live in a world where athletes, or broadcasters, for that matter, rarely perform at full strength. Isn't that all of us, no matter the profession? How often do you go to work feeling 100 percent with no distractions or anything else on your mind? Fans expect their favorite players to win, broadcasters to talk, and musicians to perform. I had offered to shorten the interview out of fear of ruining the rest of his tour, but if Tech N9ne could complete a show on one leg after feeling a pop in his calf on stage, as he recently had in St. Louis, a podcast would be a piece of cake.

"What's up, Tech?" I asked.

"What's up brother; how you doing?" the recently turned fifty-year-old replied.

Aaron Dontez Yates, a.k.a. Tech N9ne, engaged in one of my favorite podcasts of all time, talking about music, staying relevant with multiple generations, and dreams.

GAME

Among my many curiosities with Tech N9ne, the greatest involved longevity. How does a man remain relevant in a young industry more than thirty years after embarking on his career? His answer to me sounded more like a philosopher.

"I feel like life is an ever-evolving progressive thing, such as music, anything relationships, whatever you're doing. You can't be complacent."

Quite simply, Tech stays true to himself while remaining open to change. A mentor like legendary record producer Quincy Jones certainly helped mold him.

"Write what you know, and people will forever feel you," Jones told a young Tech N9ne.

"So what I did is that I've been writing my life since I've been living it. But I keep my ear to what's new, as well," meaning he's worked with Eminem, Snoop Dogg, and more recently Kendrick Lamar, and even former wrestler and movie star Dwayne "The Rock" Johnson.

He continues to adjust to the times as the beats and music evolve without getting stuck in any fad and remaining true to himself.

"I was always the weirdo with the red spiked hair, that painted face that everybody said, 'Oh, he's a devil worshiper . . . .Oh, he forgot where he came from.' Now all those people are in the crowd [screaming] 'Tech N9ne' because I stuck to my guns."

Growing up in Kansas City, the future rapper never dreamed of a music career. The philosophical side he shows as a fifty-something existed back then, with an interest in the human mind.

"I wanted to be a psychiatrist. In high school, the closest thing to it was psychology. They wouldn't give me the classes, so I stole the books and I read them at home. I just wanted to work on the thoughts of people and the feelings of people. Because I'm a people person," Tech told me.

This revelation surprised me. Most athletes I cover wanted to play professional sports growing up, yet Tech found a way into psychology through music.

"I wanted to listen to and give remedies to people in need," Tech said, but at that time, he displayed his talents as a dancer.

From rhythm, he told me, came rhyme, and he then proceeded to continue answering the question about dreams by transitioning mid-sentence into lyrics from his song "Worldwide Choppers," "Follow me all around the planet, I run the gamut on sickology. They can never manage me, we do damage with no apology," he rapped, before switching back to answering the question.

His perspective spoke to dreams changing and the purpose that can emerge during life's journeys.

"I was helping people with my thoughts," he said. "And when I would go to these towns and have meet and greets, the fans would say, 'You saved my life with this song. You saved my life with "Dysfunctional." You saved my life with "Fragile" about bullying and all this thing.' What happened was my dream as a kid to be a psychiatrist; I became my fans' psychiatrist."

I've played that clip to audiences numerous times on my speaking circuit, watching attendees realize that our dreams can change paths, but our purpose in life can help define those dreams.

Answering my podcast question about the biggest career home run, Tech listed collaborating with the Rock as a massive home run, but big picture, he reflected on connecting with entrepreneur Travis O'Guin to start an independent music label. The two met in the late 1990s and O'Guin hired the rapper to perform at a Kansas City fashion show as a brand ambassador. Blown away by Tech's performance, O'Guin discussed the possibility of further collaborating and Strange Music came to fruition in 2000.

Like any business, Strange Music suffered difficult yet important growing pains. They could count on two hands the number of people in attendance at some of the early venues. Tech says they lost $140,000 but learned a lesson in persistence, treating the minuscule group of fans like a larger crowd.

"We did that show like it was seven thousand [people]. When we came home from that tour, losing that much money, me and Trav thought we should be crazy and go back to these places. And we kept going back and when we went back the next time it was thirty people. We went back the next time, there was one hundred people. We kept going back," he said until they sold out places like House of Blues and then arenas.

Decades later, the label features more than twenty artists, including Tech N9ne.

Longtime friend Sean Tyler, who serves as communications director and artist management for Strange Music, refers to Tech as a creative genius because of his ability to take tracks, add a vision, and finish with a masterpiece for fans to play repeatedly.

"I have seen it dozens of times and am still floored at how it all came together and how he still is able to touch the souls of so many by connecting on such a personal level, even at this stage of his long career."

Another trait that led to sustained success for Tech can be found in any sports locker room, playing field, or boardroom. Name me a profession that does not reward the power of positivity. Tech N9ne brings that mindset to the stage and life wherever he goes.

"It's just energy. It's natural. For me, I'm a bright light . . . If I leave this area, you'll still see me glowing...and we spew it. Whenever we walk in the room, wherever we are, love and respect. It's good in any language."

Smiling is a universal language, and positive energy translates worldwide. I told Tech that All-Star catcher Salvador Perez, the player I've covered longer than any athlete in my career, is beloved in Kansas City. Sure, fans of the Royals love him, the native Venezuelan, for his play, but he's just as iconic for his big smile, fun-loving personality, and energy that plays in Spanish or his second language, English. The musician could relate to the athlete shining in a venue far from home.

In 2019, Tech took the stage in a small theater in Moscow, assuming ten people might be familiar with his music. But the crowd of 2,500 knew every word. Audiences in Russia, Poland, Denmark, and Switzerland all sang along to Tech's "KCMO Anthem." The musician would belt out:

"See my flag, they flyin' it, now it's no denyin' it.
Anythin' that got my city's logo, now they buyin' it.

Keep 'em goin' crazy though, TV and the radio.
Been watchin since a baby, so I'm representin' KCMO,"

And then the audience, on cue, all across the world following with "KC, MO, Roll . . . KC MO, Roll."

It reminded me of a story I heard growing up from the music we heard in my house. My parents mostly listened to classical and occasionally folk. I mostly discovered rock and hip-hop on my own and opted for Arlo Guthrie over Beethoven because it would take me becoming an adult to finally appreciate classical. So, folk it was on those long family car rides. On the Guthrie and Pete Seeger live album *More Together Again*, Guthrie spoke about a past performance in Denmark. Arlo recalled singing Elvis Presley's "Can't Help Falling in Love" with Seeger. A feeling of trepidation turned into pure bliss when he realized the audience knew every lyric, seemingly making the world a smaller place with a feel-good sing-along.

Telling that story on the live album, Guthrie said, "So there we was, thirty thousand drinking, screaming, crying, laughing, singing people, all singing an old Elvis tune somewhere in Europe. Boy, there was something wonderful about that."

The power of music or sports can bring people together, especially when accompanied by the positive vibes of a Tech N9ne. His tribute to Kansas City elicits the same reaction in rival football cities like Las Vegas and Denver.

"It's so wonderful, man. All over the world."

The dreams of Aaron Dontez Yates became a work of art for an artist who wrote what he knew, and as Quincy Jones told him, people did feel him.

POSTGAME

He's still cranking out music, appearing at sporting events, Super Bowl parades, and more. He gets the secret to life.

"I think conversation rules the nation, bro. And people don't want to talk to each other. If we didn't fear each other, we could stand near each other. And we wouldn't kill each other because we have an understanding of each other."

The world could use more people like Tech N9ne. Gone are the days of heavy partying. The lyrics chronicling those years remain, but his mission has evolved. So what more is left for a man who wants to keep working? Who or what is on his bucket list? I asked, and he pondered, admitting he'd done so much but was never satisfied. A song called "Through My Glasses" with Elton John would top his to-do list. He wrote it and sent it to the legendary artist. The premise is seeing the world through Elton and Tech's glasses, two musicians known partially for their bold attire and accessories.

If the world saw life through their glasses, "It wouldn't be war, it wouldn't be division. It would be understanding and love, and respect for all human rights. Even with different factions of religion and politics and all that, gangs, whatever it is, love and respect and understanding, through my glasses."

Will it ever happen? Who is to say no to this man who embodies the persistence, purpose, and positivity that make up dreams?

"You never know if a closed mouth don't get fed dude. You never know who's gonna respond to you, man. You never know. You have to shoot for the stars. And I've done that my whole career."

14

Freddy Fermin

PREGAME

I wrote about a young Dominican pitcher named Carlos Fortuna in my first book, *Small Ball Big Results*, and the liver cancer that would take his life at the age of twenty-three. The Kansas City Royals prospect never advanced past the lowest levels of the minor leagues due to his illness. Still, he left a legacy as the first graduate of the organization's English program that helps Latin American ballplayers learn a second language. I met and interviewed Fortuna in 2012, a year before he passed away.

Ten years later, I walked into the same Royals spring training facility in Surprise, AZ, to catch up with the big league players and get ready for the upcoming 2022 season. A minor league catcher I had never met walked up to introduce himself to me. It's not uncommon for a player I've covered for years to approach me to say hi on my first day arriving at spring training, but a young minor leaguer learning English and aspiring to one day play in the majors does not just walk up to a team broadcaster to initiate a conversation. "Hello, my name is Freddy Fermin," the catcher nervously said to me, shaking my hand. "I am learning English." He made an immediate impression, and I soon learned he was the first-ever winner of the Carlos Fortuna Award, given annually to the Royals minor league player who is most dedicated to improving his English. Fermin passed the English test that year, graduated from the program, and emerged as a reliable MLB backup to Royals legend Salvador Perez a year later.

Baseball features role players and under-the-radar success stories often hidden by the large shadows cast by superstars. Freddy Fermin epitomizes the little guy who made it against all odds. He's one of my favorite athletes I've covered in a thirty-year television career and is proof that small ball traits like hard work and persistence can make dreams come true.

GAME

Freddy Fermin first dreamed of being a baseball player as a three-year-old growing up in Venezuela. "I remember when I was a little kid, I didn't want toys for Christmas. I wanted video games to learn how to play baseball." Venezuela is known for producing some of the most talented baseball players in the world. Miguel Cabrera, Salvador Perez, and Félix Hernández have been some of MLB's biggest stars. I covered Cabrera as a Detroit Tiger for numerous games per year for sixteen seasons as he faced the Royals before retiring at the end of 2023.

There was no hitter in baseball more dangerous and feared during those years than Cabrera. I watched him become baseball's first Triple Crown winner, receiving a huge ovation on the road from Royals fans, acknowledging the moment Cabrera accomplished the rare feat. Before him, the last player to clinch the top batting average while also leading the league in home runs and RBI was Carl Yastrzemski in 1967. Hernández won a Cy Young award, two ERA titles, and threw a perfect game before retiring after 2019 as a legendary sports figure known as "King Felix" in Seattle. Salvador Perez is beloved in Kansas City and still leads the Royals. He's won five Gold Gloves, a World Series MVP, and made nine All-Star teams. I've covered Salvy longer than any athlete in my career. All three are superstars from Venezuela, and just like the previous generation of

Venezuelan icons like Omar Vizquel and Andrés Galarraga, they come from big cities like Maracay, Caracas, and Valencia.

Freddy Fermin grew up in Puerto Ordaz in the state of Bolívar, a region known for its industrial economy. "Where I come from, there aren't a lot of baseball players . . . if you want to make it, we need to work extra hard," Fermin told me.

Monica Ramirez, the Royals English instructor who plays the role of teacher, often mentor, and even second mother for the Latin American players assimilating to life in the United States, describes her students from Bolívar this way: "They all have those common traits. Humility, decent, good manners."

That describes Fermin, the son of Freddy Fermin, Sr., a manufacturing engineer. Never flashy, always polite and focused, Freddy Fermin, Jr. the big leaguer, reminds Joelvis Gonzalez of Freddy the little leaguer. Gonzalez works for the Royals in its scouting department as Venezuela Supervisor. He first laid eyes on Fermin as a seven-year-old catcher and second baseman. When games ended and kids scattered around the park to play soccer and run around, Freddy remained at the field, watching every pitch of the next game, wanting more. "Always the best hitter on the team. Hungry to play. Always serious and focused. Freddy is the same guy . . . Freddy has been serious since he was a child," Gonzalez told me. He was serious and focused then, just as he would be in 2024, logging significant playing time on a Royals team that made the playoffs for the first time since 2015. That was also the year Freddy's unthinkable professional journey began.

Gonzalez's job as a scout involves finding players in Venezuela and recommending the kids with potential to be signed. Part of his role involves building relationships with families well before they are eligible to sign with MLB organizations at the age of sixteen. Gonzalez describes his connection with the Fermins as special. He played a significant role in the unlikely success story of a catcher considered too small and too old to attract attention.

Back in 2015, Freddy's brother Edgardo was set to sign a contract with the New York Mets, opening a path for the younger sibling to join the franchise's Dominican Academy in 2015. As a fifteen-year-old, Edgardo would move to the Dominican prior to signing at sixteen and start living, working out, and playing with other Latin Americans, hopeful to earn a career in professional baseball. At nineteen, Freddy's window to attract interest barely remained open. Still, Edgardo convinced his big brother to travel to the Dominican to try out for the Mets with the hope that they might sign him to a contract as well. The Mets did not like what they saw, so Freddy tried asking other teams for a tryout. The Miami Marlins agreed, but after multiple days of showing up at their academy and being told each time to "come back tomorrow," an upset Freddy decided to move on.

Fermin was ready to head home, but Gonzalez asked him to wait before returning to Venezuela. The scout planned to travel to the Dominican Republic in ten days to help coach at the Royals Academy, and he thought he could convince the team to take a look at Freddy.

Needing somewhere to stay in the interim, Fermin ended up living temporarily at what Gonzalez described as "an ugly place," with bad conditions in Santo Domingo, the Capital city of the Dominican Republic. Others described it as basically "living on the street." A cheap room in a dilapidated building with cracked walls, crumbling stairs, and meals of spaghetti with liver enabled Freddy to survive. Fermin reluctantly talked to me about the memory, not because of the awful conditions but because complaining would minimize people in a worse situation back in Venezuela. And he still held on to a sliver of hope. "I had to put up with it until the angel Joelvis showed up," Fermin said.

Freddy's worried father would call Joelvis every day. "When are you getting there? How much longer," until he finally arrived and made his pitch to the Royals. The only problem was the Royals did not need a catcher. Gonzales said to Victor Baez, the Royals Dominican Academy Field coordinator, "I know we are late, but he's better than all the catchers that we have."

As a favor to Gonzalez, the Royals decided to allow him to stay and work out with the team until he found transportation back to Venezuela. Baez says they told Fermin: "You can stay here with us, but we need to be honest with you. We don't have a spot for you here."

Freddy just wanted a chance and told Baez, "If I don't play good, I will leave. Let me play. I don't need a lot of money. Give me a chance."

After watching the small catcher, Baez thought, "Oh my God, this kid is really mature. He's really hungry." No one worked harder. The Royals staff saw talent and a work ethic that stood above the competition. As players went back to their rooms to rest following a workout, one kid stayed and watched every pitch and then dissected the action with the staff at the end. This is what Gonzalez already knew and that the Royals needed to see, what Joelvis first saw on the little league fields of Venezuela. It's what Monica Ramirez would eventually notice once Freddy made it to the United States as a Royals minor leaguer and the way he craved learning a new language so he could better communicate with the pitchers he caught. She remembers first meeting him in her class in Arizona. "All newbies sit near me, but he sat further away because the ones from Bolívar are more quiet . . . He was super serious." Fermin approached the woman he simply calls "Teacher" to this day after class and asked for extra sessions. "He wouldn't leave me alone," she said, laughing with admiration.

He made it to the US because of what he showed the decision-makers at the Dominican Academy. Latin American teenagers who sign with an MLB team start at the club's Dominican Academy, where they live, study, practice, and play baseball in the Dominican Summer League, which is the lowest level of minor league ball. However, prior to signing, the youngest players compete against other teams at an informal introductory level called the Tricky League. That's where they put Freddy to play while he stayed at the Academy, competing against much younger talent like future MLB stars Juan Soto and Vladimir Guerrero, Jr.

In his first game, Freddy went 4-4. "I was working so hard. They started talking about me; wow," Freddy recalled. Four hits in four at-bats before leaving after the eighth inning with cramps that sent him to the training room. Fabio Herrera, the Royals Manager of International Operations, who works at the Academy, remembers Fermin suffering from dehydration. He was exhausted from working too hard, and he needed to be transported to the hospital to receive fluids intravenously. Herrera recognized the hard-nosed and tough mentality of Fermin, who had not slowed down on the field all day. "He always has that 'I can do more mentality,' and from that day, you could tell he was that type of guy," Herrera said.

The next day, Freddy told the trainers, "I'm ready to go back in," only to be disappointed by the instruction that he was not allowed to play. Upset at yet another perceived setback, a disappointed Fermin wondered why, without realizing what would come next.

Baez said everyone fell in love with Fermin's skills and work ethic from the moment he took the field for that 4-4 game in the Tricky League. The staff called Rene Francisco, the Royals Senior Vice President of International Operations. Baez remembers the message for the longtime Royals executive. "This kid that the scout left at the academy . . . We think that he is better than all the catchers we have here."

The Royals did not want Fermin to play the day after his visit to the hospital because they wanted him to take a physical and sign a contract. They cut one of the other catchers and gave him ten thousand dollars. Freddy called his girlfriend Consuela, the woman who he began dating in 2013 and who he would marry in 2018. Consuela always encouraged him. He then called his family and celebrated on a video call with his mom Zenaida. "I was really happy and very emotional and sentimental at the same time."

The pattern of being overlooked or underestimated continued. Many Latin Americans play in winter leagues after their MLB or minor league seasons end to stay fresh during the offseason. However, no team in the Venezuelan Winter League signed him for the 2021-2022 season, so he played in Panama instead. A year later, they took notice. Fermin won the Venezuelan League Most Valuable Player award, and he was a unanimous selection for Rookie of the Year. Every step along the way came with overcoming adversity.

When higher-paid players received more opportunities, Joelvis Gonzalez reminded Fermin of his resilience and reliability. He told him baseball is a business and to just keep putting up numbers and grinding. He used the analogy of a car when sharing motivation with Freddy. "If you've got a Mustang, if you've got a Rolls Royce, and you've got a Toyota Corolla, you've got to show your expensive cars." Meaning those other prospects with higher signing bonuses represented the fancy cars. Freddy was the Corolla. "You are the Corolla. You are doing your job, but you're not the main piece right now."

The reliable Corolla arrived for a test drive in 2022, playing in three games for the Royals. A year later, Fermin logged seventy games, backing up his hero Salvador Perez. Anytime I looked up and saw Salvy on the road walking into the hotel or getting off the team bus, Freddy was a few steps behind him, following the Rolls Royce of the Royals. "I remember when I was at the tryout, I saw Salvador Perez, and now I'm next to him. It's incredible to play with Salvador. It's surreal."

In 2024 Fermin emerged as one of the Royals best hitters, and one of MLB's best defensive catchers. It allowed Perez to play first base more to rest his body while making sure the franchise did not miss the elite level of defense from the longtime superstar. The Corolla fit in right alongside the Rolls, performing with the steady and reliable nature that embodies Freddy Fermin.

POSTGAME

Freddy Fermin joined my broadcast partner Jeff Montgomery and me on April 25, 2023, as a guest on our pregame show in front of the visiting dugout at Chase Field in Phoenix. He found the courage to answer questions on live television without a translator, an uncommon occurrence for a player learning English. But it was no different than the strength he showed asking for a chance with the Royals back at the Dominican Academy, or introducing himself to me at spring training. This is one of the many reasons teammates, coaches, staff, and media all respect Freddy. After the pregame show appearance, Salvador Perez told all the Royals Spanish-speaking players in the clubhouse to start using their English more in interviews. "If Freddy can do it, you can do it." And they did.

Fermin has impressed people during every step of the journey because of his ability to play small ball. Monica Ramirez remembers his first MLB game. "When he made his debut in the majors in Toronto, I cried, and I never cry . . . this is why you work so hard and you give them so much time. Hard work does pay off."

Joelvis Gonzalez, the scout and longtime family friend, still receives regular calls from the twenty-nine-year-old Fermin, asking for advice on baseball and life. Gonzalez admitted to me, "I feel so proud. I'm not going to lie. Sometimes I cry watching Freddy play in the big leagues."

I passed these messages on to Fermin and shared my own admiration for him, and he replied like the humble, focused, and serious kid Gonzalez still sees today. "Wow. I feel like I'm not done yet. I'm in big league ball. I want more."

Someone will doubt him, but they shouldn't. Fermin is a player who will never stop pushing.

Epilogue

I will never forget the final Friday of September 2024, a historic night for the Kansas City Royals. After losing to the Braves in Atlanta, KC waited with champagne ready on ice. While they had preferred to clinch their first playoff berth in nine years by winning that night's game, they would still make the playoffs with a loss by rival Minnesota, who eventually did lose at home in Minneapolis about an hour and a half after the Royals finished.

While the team sat in the clubhouse in anticipation of a party, my longtime broadcast partner Jeff Montgomery and I filled the time with an extended postgame show, talking live for nearly an hour and a half, about three times longer than a usual show. When I dreamed of being a broadcaster, the thought of hosting a live television show and filling time for more than an hour never crossed my mind, but I know when I began my career, just making it through a five-minute sportscast tested my nerves. Nearly thirty years later, Monty and I cruised through the show with our producer, John Harvey, leading the way. Total comfort in the task at hand felt like validation earned from a long career of experience. It was a dream come true. Keeping Kansas City fans entertained while they waited to watch their team bask in the glory of incredible accomplishment felt like a privilege. My dream was always to tell people stories and take them places they may not get to go. We brought them to Atlanta via the magic of television. As I entered the clubhouse shortly after Minnesota lost, I knew I could take fans to the party as the Royals became the first team in Major League Baseball history to make it to the playoffs a year after losing 106 games.

I've covered numerous champagne celebrations, dating back to my years as a sportscaster in St. Louis, and have always enjoyed these moments as much as any in baseball. Grown men spraying champagne and dumping beers make for fun television. My usual star-of-the-game interviews focus more on the details of a specific game. Cliches can be more common as players are more focused on the day-to-day happenings of the sport. Such is the life of the baseball grind. But playoff celebrations bring out the most fun personalities, and the athletes always enjoy dousing their team broadcaster with celebratory suds. As I walked through the clubhouse with my cameraman at my side, I waved over the only player in uniform who took part in the last Royals postseason party, a World Series winner in 2015. Most of the players on that team were now retired, enjoying life after seeing their baseball dreams come true. All that remained was Salvador Perez, the Royals catcher, team captain, and future Hall of Famer who was completing one of his best seasons yet, a renaissance of sorts, at the age of thirty-four.

I first interviewed Salvy, a twenty-year-old minor leaguer, during spring training for a story about top prospects.

The Venezuelan-born kid learning English walked my way and said, "Easy questions, sir, easy questions."

I've now covered Salvy longer than any athlete in my career and consider him a friend, as much as such a thing exists between a player and broadcaster. No one works harder, players say, than Salvador Perez. I respect his space and his need to work hard and prepare to perform every day, and he knows I need to do my job and report on the team and its players. But the fun we've had in interviews and around the ballpark is unlike anything I've experienced with any other player.

At the end of the 2023 season, Salvy found out that my wife Susan and I would soon pass through Miami on a trip to South America. He and his wife make South Florida their home in the offseason, and Salvy invited us to spend a day with him on his boat. I thought he was messing with me, as our friendship never involved time away from work. He meant it and picked us up from the airport, showed us the city by boat, and put us up for the night. I noticed he was the same guy away from the ballpark with all the same characteristics that make him one of MLB's most beloved personalities and respected players.

Passion, immense pride, attention to detail, and a true love of life: "Mama, look at the dolphins," he said to Susan with the same big grin he flashed on the baseball diamond, chatting up anyone and everyone.

I looked at him and asked, "Ever dream of this growing up in Venezuela?"

"Never," he told me.

I thought about this as the thirty-four-year-old approached me for the live interview in the partying clubhouse. The players on the Royals said they won it for Salvy.

I would get to that question, but I could see what was about to happen, so I began the interview by saying, "Oh no, I know what you're up to," as Salvy dumped a full bottle of champagne over my head on live TV.

"Jooooooel, you're part of it too. Jooooooooel," he yelled, dumping the final drops on my head before I caught my breath and proceeded with the interview.

As the champagne dripped from my nose, I asked him what the moment meant to him, and he spoke about how excited he was for the young guys. He was happy to lead the future generation of players.

As for his long career and dreams, Salvy said, "I'm not twenty-four anymore, but I want to play until I'm forty-five if I can," he said.

A coach poured a beer over the hood that covered Salvy's head. The superstar shook off the beer, thanked me with an already hoarse voice, and walked off to celebrate with his teammates before returning to work in pursuit of more dreams. I moved on to the next interview, living my dreams, too.

Acknowledgments

truly believe I have the best job in the world. Sometimes during a losing streak or a tough season like the Kansas City Royals 106-loss campaign in 2023, friends, relatives, or fans will check in on me to see if I'm doing all right.

My sincere response is, "Don't worry about me. I get paid to talk about baseball every day. I'm living my dream."

Sure, winning is always more fun, but I refuse to let the result of a game bring me down when I have the privilege of working in baseball and coming into fans' homes via our broadcast every night. It's not always easy, but my dream is a reality due to the support of my family.

Susan has lived the life of a baseball wife for decades while being the rock of our family. No one in the world has been a bigger cheerleader for me than her, and I'm so grateful to be on this journey with a strong and independent woman who understands that summer vacations and weekends off are not part of the equation. We are a family of three for half of the year until I reemerge after baseball season, and it works during the season and offseason because Mason and Ellie have a present mom. I'm not sure if Susan knew what she was getting into when we started dating in 1995. I'm pretty sure she hoped that the sports reporter working for the NBC television affiliate in Rhinelander, Wisconsin, would move on to bigger markets. Still, neither of us knew we would end up in Kansas City, where she grew up until the age of eleven.

Our kids were born in St. Louis, my previous market, but they were raised in KC. Five-year-old Mason and two-year-old Ellie made the move when I switched to the Royals, and it's been one of the joys of my life watching them both grow up, attending the local schools from kindergarten through high school in a city we proudly called home.

Mason now attends the University of Kansas, sharing my love of sports and the gift of gab. He inspires me every day with his kindness and his ability to battle adversity.

Ellie was our firecracker from day one, appropriate as a Fourth of July baby. She's our actress, comedian, and student who strives for perfection every day. I'm not sure who she got that from, but I would guess her mother. I'm proud of our theater kid and love watching her thrive at DePaul in Chicago.

These three and our dogs, Maggie and Sienna, are my everything. Of course, our supportive families and friends on both sides are instrumental in my living this dream, and I thank them all.

As far as work, I hired Ashleigh Sterr a few years back to be my executive assistant, podcast producer, and anything else involving my many endeavors. She's the most organized person I know, my sounding board and confidant with this book, and I could not run my speaking business while focusing on television without her help. I knew when I hired her I would have the perfect complement to my free-wheeling, spontaneous way of operating because her father, Jeff Montgomery, is extremely organized and the yin to my yang. The apple rarely falls far from the tree. There's a reason Monty and I have been television partners without one argument or bad day for the last fifteen seasons. I take pride in our chemistry and it's fun now to watch his daughter work with me and my daughter babysit Ashleigh's kids. Ashleigh's younger sister Katy used to babysit for Mason and Ellie. The Montgomerys are family.

Our Royals television crew is amazing, and I love working with them all. Our longtime director, Steve Kurtenbach, and game producer, Kevin Cedergren, lead a group of talented and passionate men and women. Monty and I have had several excellent producers over the years. John Harvey has produced our *Royals Live* pregame and postgame shows in recent seasons, and "Harv" is as good as anyone we've ever had. Monty, Harv, and I click on all fronts, making television easy and fun. I can speak for Monty in saying we are lucky to work with Harv.

Sharing airtime and charter planes and bus rides with our TV game announcers Ryan Lefebvre, Rex Hudler, Jake Eisenberg, and Steve Physioc before Jake has been a career highlight. I've heard Hud say many times, "We lead the league in laughs." We spend more time with each other than our families for half the year and I consider them all my friends.

Covering Royals baseball is different from what many of my broadcasting peers experience. I know they all love their jobs, but the Royals franchise treats us like family, and that's not common in our industry. It starts with team owner John Sherman and includes Royals Vice President and General Manager JJ Picollo, the front office, manager Matt Quatraro, his coaching staff, and the athletes. Ballplayers have come and gone over the years, but they've all been respectful. From the Hall of Famer George Brett to current star Salvador Perez and everyone in between, they have always been good to me. Part of living dreams and playing small ball involves treating people right, respecting boundaries and space, building trust, and being fair. I try to do that every day and am forever thankful to all of these players who treat a non-athlete like me with respect.

We are also so fortunate to have a supportive media relations staff who make our lives easier every day. Sam Mellinger and his team of Nick Kappel, Ian Kraft, and Logan Jones are the best at what they do.

Thanks to my longtime TV colleague, podcast editor, and friend, Colleen Lotz. I trust her with any work she does and am lucky to have known Colleen for twenty years. I love working with my speaking manager, Charlotte Raybourn, as well as Kendall Jackson, who handles my podcast and speaking promotions on social media. I'm also grateful for the partnerships with Community America Credit Union and Chief of Staff Kansas City.

I self-published my first book, *Small Ball Big Results*, during the pandemic. *Small Ball Big Dreams* took more energy as attempting to tell these stories during the grind of two baseball seasons made for a slow process. I could not do this project without Indie Books International, led by Henry DeVries and Devin DeVries.

And finally, a huge thank you to baseball fans in Kansas City, around the country, and around the world. It's truly an honor and a privilege to bring you these stories while living my dream.

About the Author

Joel Goldberg is an Emmy Award-winning broadcaster, long-time television host, and reporter traveling with the Kansas City Royals. He lives in Kansas City with his wife, Susan, where they raised their two children, Mason and Ellie.

Joel is the author of the book *Small Ball Big Results* and hosts the podcast *Rounding The Bases*. He also runs a speaking company, delivering keynotes titled "Winning Trust" and "Breaking Barriers in the Ballpark Change," and his culture speech called "Small Ball Big Results."

For more information, please visit www.joelgoldbergmedia.com.

www.ingramcontent.com/pod-product-compliance
Lightning Source LLC
Chambersburg PA
CBHW031941190326
41519CB00007B/608